JOURNEY TO
MATURITY

NAVIGATING YOUNG ADULTHOOD
WITH RESILIENCE AND GRACE

BEN POVLOW

Journey To Maturity

Navigating Young Adulthood with
Resilience and Grace

Ben Povlow

The Self-Help Company, LLC.

Also by Ben Povlow

Self-Help for At-Risk Teens: Overcome the Odds and
Live the Life of Your Dreams

The Young Adult Starter Kit: 12 Steps To Being A
Better Person

Check Out
Ben's Podcast

RAISING YOURSELF UP

WITH HOST **BEN POVLOW**

Available in all major podcast directories

Dedication

I dedicate this book to all of my mentors. Including those of you who I only know through your books, videos, and audio training. Your wisdom, guidance, and inspiration have made me the person I am today.

To my friend, Dwayne Golden. Thank you for being a great example of what it means to live with faith and dignity.

Contents

Introduction   1

Chapter 1   3
The Importance of Continuous Learning and Upgrading
Skills

Chapter 2   12
The Crossroads of Young Adulthood

Chapter 3   20
The Role of Vulnerability

Chapter 4   28
From Passion to Profession

Chapter 5   37
Travel, Explore, and Expand Your Horizons

Chapter 6   45
Social Media and Mental Health

Chapter 7   53
Financial Literacy

Chapter 8   61
Relationships

Chapter 9   69
Dealing with Failure and Rejection

Chapter 10   77
The Value of Mentorship

Chapter 11   85
Legacy Thinking

Chapter 12   94
Embracing Change

Chapter 13   102
Nurturing Creativity

Chapter 14   110
Networking and Building Authentic Connections

Chapter 15   118
Civic Responsibility

Chapter 16   127
Time Management

Chapter 17   135
Health and Wellness

Chapter 18   143
The Joy of Giving

Chapter 19   150
Personal Branding

Chapter 20   158
Building a Support System

Afterword   167

About The Author   168

Introduction

J ourney to Maturity: Navigating Young Adulthood with Resilience and Grace is more than just a book; it's a compass for
the intricate journey of young adulthood. This phase of life is filled
with a whirlwind of emotions, decisions, and discoveries. It's a time
when one grapples with questions about career, relationships, and
self-identity. While this can be a period of joy and exploration, it's also
often accompanied by uncertainties and challenges.

I wrote this book to guide and support young adults through this
transformative phase using a storytelling approach. In a way that's
different from my previous books, I share wisdom, experiences, and
practical advice, hoping to illuminate the path for those who might
feel lost or overwhelmed. The book touches upon various essential
aspects of adulthood, from understanding emotions and building
meaningful relationships to financial literacy and personal growth.

Life is about thriving, not just surviving. Every challenge is an
opportunity to learn and grow with resilience and grace. This book's
narrative is heartfelt, aiming to resonate with readers, letting them
know they aren't alone in their journey. Through my words, I aspire
to empower young adults to navigate their path with confidence, optimism, and a sense of purpose.

Let's begin the Journey to Maturity.

Chapter 1

Learning had a definitive beginning and end in a quaint corner of history. It started in childhood and continued through school and college, and by the time one entered the realm of adulthood, it was thought that the education phase of one's life was over. However, the world we live in today is different. It's a dynamic, evolving entity where change is the only constant, and in this kaleidoscope of rapid transformations, the traditional approach to learning needs to be revised.

The bedrock of modern existence is innovation. With the blink of an eye, industries revolutionize, technologies evolve, and skills once hailed as crucial become obsolete. In such a world, can learning be confined to the formative years? Not. Lifelong learning isn't just a fancy term coined by modern philosophers; it's a necessity, a survival tool, and an armor that shields and propels individuals in this age of relentless evolution.

To paint a clearer picture, consider the digital revolution. Two decades ago, the idea of smart homes, voice assistants, or augmented reality was the stuff of science fiction. Today, they're our reality. Someone who finished formal education in the 90s without a commitment to continuous learning would find themselves stranded in the face of today's technological advancements.

But it's not just about technology. The sociocultural fabric of society is evolving too. Ideas, beliefs, and norms once set in stone are now being questioned, refined, and redefined. As global migration increases and cultures intertwine, understanding and empathy become crucial. Again, continuous learning about the world and its myriad hues plays a pivotal role.

The modern job market is a fluid entity. The career paths that seemed secure a few decades ago are undergoing seismic shifts. Many roles are being automated, and new ones are emerging. In this flux, the only way to stay relevant is to embrace a perpetual growth and learning mindset.

Lifelong learning, however, is about more than just professional relevance. It's a treasure trove of personal enrichment. Think about the sheer joy of picking up a musical instrument in your 40s, discovering the magic of painting in your 60s, or mastering a new language in your 50s. Learning keeps the mind agile, the heart young, and the soul enriched. It adds layers to existence, making life a rich array of experiences.

But how does one keep the flame of curiosity alive in the hustle and bustle of life? The first step is to redefine the concept of learning. It's not confined to classrooms, textbooks, or certificates. The world is a school; every experience is a lesson, and every individual is a potential teacher. When we view life through this lens, every moment becomes an opportunity for growth.

Staying updated in one's professional field is, of course, crucial. But equally important at any age is the willingness to learn from everything. Books, for instance, are portals to different worlds. They offer wisdom, perspectives, and insights, making them an invaluable resource. Similarly, travel, even if it's just to a neighboring town, is a lesson in geography, culture, and humanity.

With all its challenges, the digital age also offers unparalleled learning avenues. Online courses, webinars, and YouTube have made continuing education easier than ever. No longer is learning confined to brick-and-mortar institutions. The best minds, and the most prestigious universities, are now available with a button click.

Discussion groups, both online and offline, are another potent tool. They provide platforms to share, debate, and refine ideas, leading to a holistic understanding. Similarly, mentoring—both being a mentor and seeking one—can be incredibly enlightening. It offers firsthand insights into experiences, mistakes, and learnings that textbooks often overlook.

Yet, the cornerstone of lifelong learning is a shift in mindset. Learning is about celebrating questions as much as answers. It's about viewing mistakes as lessons, not failures. It's about having the humility to accept that no matter how much one knows, there's always more to learn.

In this rapidly changing world, the arc of learning can never really come full circle. Life is an eternal classroom, and we are the students. By embracing lifelong learning, we equip ourselves to navigate the waves of change and add depth, joy, and richness to our journey. Mahatma Gandhi said, "Live each day as if it were your last. As though you were going to live forever, learn."

Sources for Continuous Education

The pursuit of knowledge is an eternal journey, one that enriches our lives both personally and professionally. As the world becomes more interconnected and information becomes more accessible, continuous education has evolved from a luxury to a necessity. Yet, while the desire to learn might be innate, the path to constant education can seem overwhelming. With countless resources, both online and offline, where does one begin? How do we chart a course in this vast ocean of information?

Let's demystify a common misconception: continuous education is not synonymous with formal schooling. While traditional educational institutions are a valuable source, they are a single star in a vast constellation of learning.

The Library: The Age-Old Repository of Knowledge

Libraries, often viewed as relics of a bygone era, remain one of the most comprehensive sources of knowledge. Beyond books, modern libraries have adapted to the digital age, providing access to e-books, online journals, and databases. They often host talks, workshops, and discussion groups, turning them into community hubs of learning and networking. Whether diving deep into a specific subject or browsing the aisles, libraries offer a serene environment for reflection and study.

Online Courses and Platforms: The Digital Classroom

The internet has transformed education. Platforms like Coursera, Udemy, and Khan Academy provide courses on everything from quantum physics to digital marketing. Prestigious institutions like Harvard, Stanford, and MIT offer free online courses, bridging the gap between elite education and global accessibility. These platforms provide:

Flexibility.

Allowing you to learn at your pace.

Revisiting lectures and adjusting your schedule as needed.

Workshops and Seminars: The Interactive Experience

Workshops and seminars, often hosted by experts in the field, offer an interactive learning experience. They provide hands-on training, real-world problem-solving, and the opportunity to engage in discussions. Beyond knowledge, they provide the invaluable benefit of networking and connecting participants with industry peers and experts.

Travel: The World as Your Classroom

Travel, both domestic and international, offers education in its rawest form. It teaches you about history, culture, geography, and human nature. Every trip, and every interaction is a lesson in diversity, adaptability, and empathy. While not traditional education, the wisdom gained from travel is profound, shaping your worldview and personal ethos.

Podcasts and Webinars: Learning on the Go

In today's fast-paced world, finding time can be a challenge. Enter podcasts and webinars. Whether commuting, exercising, or doing household chores, you can join discussions on your favorite subjects. They offer insights, interviews, and debates, covering many topics and turning idle time into productive learning.

Community College and Evening Classes

Community colleges and evening classes are an amazing resource for those who yearn for a classroom experience. They provide structured learning without the long-term commitment of a degree program. Whether it's science, coding, or a foreign language, these institutions cater to diverse interests, often at affordable rates.

Museums and Cultural Centers

Art, history, science, and culture come alive in museums. They offer a visual and often interactive experience, providing context and depth to the information. On the other hand, cultural centers offer immersion in art forms, traditions, and crafts. From theater, to dance to artisanal workshops, they celebrate heritage and creativity.

Mentorship: Wisdom Beyond Books

While information can be gleaned from books and lectures, wisdom often comes from experience. Seeking a mentor in your field of interest provides practical and profound insights. It's a relationship beyond education, offering guidance, support, and perspective.

Discussion Groups and Book Clubs: The Power of Collective Learning

Learning is as much about listening as it's about speaking. Discussion groups and book clubs offer a platform for both. They foster a debate, discussion, and reflection culture, turning individual insights into collective wisdom.

Self-Study: The Unstructured Path

Last but not least, never underestimate the power of self-study. With the internet at your fingertips, the world is your oyster. Dive into online articles, academic papers, and forums, or pick up a book. Set your own pace, chart your course, and let your curiosity be your guide.

In conclusion, the avenues for continuous education are diverse and abundant. It's a buffet of knowledge waiting to be savored. The trick is to continue to be interested, flexible, and proactive. In the words of Albert Einstein, "Once you stop learning, you start dying." In this information age, let's pledge to be eternal students, forever hungry for knowledge and perpetually young in the heart.

Balancing Work and Study

For many, the challenge of balancing work and study can feel like trying to stand on a seesaw without it tilting. On one end, there's the pressing need to earn and sustain oneself, and on the other, the desire to grow, learn, and secure a brighter future. Balancing these two demanding aspects of life can be challenging, but it's not impossible.

Picture this: Emily, a young aspiring psychologist, works 9-to-5 at a city firm. She's buried in textbooks by evening, preparing for her postgraduate exams. She often finds herself overwhelmed, juggling client meetings and class assignments while maintaining her social life. Like many in her shoes, the struggle is real, but so is the dream.

So, how does one navigate this intricate dance between professional demands and academic aspirations? Let's delve deeper into Emily's life and extract some insights.

Understanding the "Why"

Before diving headfirst into this dual journey, Emily took a moment to reflect. She asked herself why she wanted to pursue further studies. Was it passion, a desire for a higher salary, or perhaps a combination? By understanding her motivations, Emily was better equipped to push through the inevitable late nights and early mornings. She kept a picture of her dream university and a vision board in her room, serving as daily reminders of her end goal.

Planning Ahead

Sunday evenings became Emily's planning sanctuary. She would sit down with her planner, marking out work commitments, study schedules, assignment deadlines, and even penciling in breaks and leisure time. This proactive approach eliminated last-minute chaos and allowed her to prepare for the week's demands in advance.

Setting Boundaries

Emily needed to separate work from the study. When at her job, her focus was solely on her tasks, not the upcoming test or paper she had to write. Conversely, when studying, she wasn't contemplating work emails. Establishing these clear boundaries increased her efficiency in both arenas.

Efficient Time Management

Emily realized early on that it's not about your hours, but how you use them. She adopted the Pomodoro Technique, which demands complete concentration for 25 minutes and then taking a 5-minute break. This method helped her retain information better and reduce the fatigue of prolonged study sessions.

Seeking Support

Sharing her journey with close friends and family, Emily was met with an outpouring of support. They understood when she couldn't attend social events or needed quiet for a study session. She also joined study groups and online forums where she connected with others on a similar journey. Their shared experiences, tips, and encouragement were invaluable.

Self-Care is Not Selfish

Amidst the hustle, Emily never forgot to care for herself. She ensured she slept well, ate balanced meals, and incorporated short workouts into her routine. These not only kept her physically fit but mentally agile too. Occasionally, she'd indulge in a spa day or a night out with friends to rejuvenate and refresh her spirit.

Flexibility Over Rigidity

While planning was essential, Emily also recognized the importance of being flexible. Sometimes work emergencies arose, or she needed extra study time for a challenging topic. She learned to adjust her schedule, swapping study sessions or taking short breaks without guilt.

Celebrating Small Wins

She celebrated each time Emily aced a test or completed a challenging work project. These small rewards, be it a treat, a quick trip, or a day off, motivated her to keep pushing forward.

Facing Failures

Not every test was a success, and not every workday was smooth. Emily faced her fair share of setbacks. However, instead of dwelling on them, she learned from her experiences. Analyzing her mistakes, seeking feedback, and adapting her strategies, she turned each failure into a stepping stone.

As the months passed, Emily began mastering the art of balancing work and study. It wasn't easy, but she found her rhythm with grit, determination, and a clear vision. Her journey wasn't about sacrificing one for the other, but about harmonizing them to create a melody of personal and professional growth.

While balancing work and study is undoubtedly challenging, it's a journey that fosters growth, resilience, and a profound understanding of one's strengths and weaknesses. And for those willing to embark on this path, like Emily, the tangible and intangible rewards are worth every ounce of effort.

Chapter 2

The transition from teenage years to adulthood is powerful experience. Much like the captivating transformation of a caterpillar into a butterfly, this phase of our lives is marked by intense growth, change, and emergence into a new realm of experiences and responsibilities. While both stages of life have their joys, challenges, and moments of thoughtfulness, the leap from being a teen to an adult is worth the growing pains.

The teenage years, swirling with a whirlwind of emotions, hormonal changes, and an innate quest for identity, are a period of exploration. During these years, one is often sheltered within the cocoon of parental guidance and the relatively fixed structure of school life. There's comfort in routine; school, extracurricular activities, spending time with friends, family vacations, and those occasional rebellious acts that become anecdotes in our adult lives. The world feels expansive, but our corner is snug and defined.

As the teen years wind down and the phase of adulthood approaches, the cocoon unfolds. The protective barriers, once comforting, may start to feel restrictive. A new horizon of possibilities awaits, and with it comes the realization of independence. This is where recognizing the shift is crucial.

One of the most obvious signs of this shift is the weight of decision-making. As teens, most decisions, from what to eat for dinner to which subjects to study, often have the cushion of parental input or are influenced by peer opinion. In contrast, adulthood brings with it the autonomy of choice. These choices, whether related to higher education, career, relationships, or lifestyle, have repercussions and rewards. It's exhilarating and daunting simultaneously, as each option seems to shape the path ahead.

The nature of relationships also transforms. In school, friendships are formed on shared timetables, lunch breaks, and class projects. With its varied commitments and schedules, adulthood requires more intentional effort to sustain connections. Relationships evolve to encompass not just camaraderie but also deeper emotional and often financial responsibilities. From considering moving in with a partner to managing one's finances, relationships in adulthood demand maturity and understanding.

Likewise, the realization of time's fleeting nature becomes more pronounced. As teenagers, summers seemed endless, and waiting for a milestone age, like 18 or 21, felt like an eternity. However, in adulthood, time takes on a different tempo. Days turn into months, and months into years, with a swiftness that often takes us by surprise. This awareness underscores the importance of time management, prioritization, balancing work, relaxation, personal growth, and relationships.

Another noteworthy aspect is the confrontation with the concept of 'self.' Teenagers often grapple with identity, influenced heavily by peers, popular culture, and societal norms. However, as adults, the journey becomes more introspective. There's a search for purpose, values, beliefs, and a personal brand of identity detached from external validation. This introspection can lead to moments of solitude, self-doubt, and existential questions, but it's also the foundation upon which the adult self is constructed.

Amidst these seismic shifts, there lies the essence of continuity. Our teenage years, with their lessons, memories, and experiences, don't vanish. They merge into our adult lives, coloring our perceptions, decisions, and interactions. Recognizing the shift from teen to adult is not about discarding the past, but integrating it into our evolving narrative.

The journey from adolescence to adulthood is a rite of passage. It's a dance of change, constancy, and newfound freedoms and responsibilities. Recognizing this shift is the first step in embracing the beauty, challenges, and growth that adulthood promises. As we navigate this journey, we must remember that every adult was once a teen, uncertain about the future. And just as the past has shaped us, our actions and choices today will mold the adults we continue to become.

Overcoming Uncertainty

In the vast, ever-changing landscape of life, if one constant companion walks alongside every individual, it's the shadow of uncertainty. It's that niggling feeling in the back of your mind, the tightening in your chest, the questions that keep you up at 3 am. As we transition from one phase of life to another, particularly from the cocooned world of adolescence to the expansive realm of adulthood, uncertainty only seems to grow in size and intensity. Yet, how we respond to this uncertainty, rather than its mere existence, defines our experiences, growth, and future.

The roots of uncertainty are deep-seated and wide-ranging. They could arise from financial challenges, career choices, relationships, or the general direction of life. Often, it stems from the fear of the unknown, the spaces in our life map where the path hasn't been charted yet. During such times, it's natural to feel like you're standing at the edge of a cliff, wind howling around you, with no clear sign of what lies ahead.

Herein lies the first step to overcoming uncertainty: acknowledging it. By accepting that uncertainty is an inevitable aspect of life and not something to be ashamed of or shunned, we can start to face it head-on. Think of it like standing in a dark room. Initially, the darkness is overwhelming. But the longer you stand, the more your eyes adjust, and soon, you begin to discern shapes, objects, and the way forward.

Engaging with our uncertainties rather than running away allows us to understand their nature. You may be uncertain about a career choice because you're not fully informed. Or the uncertainty about a relationship stems from unresolved feelings or conversations. Engaging with our apprehension's source helps clarify it, making the unknown a little more known.

One of the most empowering approaches to dealing with uncertainty is cultivating a future facing mindset. This involves viewing challenges as opportunities to learn and evolve rather than insurmountable hurdles. By adopting a mindset of growth, we can approach the uncertainties of life with curiosity.

Rather than viewing a situation as failure, choose to ask, "What can I learn from this experience?".

Remember that it's okay to seek help. External perspectives often provide clarity, whether it's confiding in a trusted friend, seeking the counsel of a mentor, or getting professional guidance from a therapist or coach. Sometimes, articulating our uncertainties can illuminate them, making them less daunting.

Another critical factor in overcoming uncertainty is building resilience. Life will always throw curveballs our way. Strength doesn't mean not feeling the impact; it means bouncing back, learning from the experience, and forging ahead with a renewed sense of purpose. This resilience is built over time through facing and overcoming challenges and continually reinforcing the belief in oneself.

Grounding practices can also play an essential role in navigating through uncertain times. This could be in meditation, journaling, spending time in nature, or any other activity that provides a sense of stability and connection to oneself. Such practices anchor, giving solace and perspective in turbulent times.

While the future remains a realm of the unknown, focusing on the present is helpful. In the words of renowned spiritual teacher Eckhart Tolle, "The present moment is all you ever have." By anchoring ourselves in the now and being fully engaged in our current tasks, relationships, and experiences, we reduce the anxiety stemming from the uncertainties of the future. This doesn't mean not planning for the future, but rather, not getting so lost in the 'what ifs' that we forget to live today.

Consider becoming comfortable with the journey of uncertainty. Every individual, at various junctures in their life, grapples with it. The paths of life are not linear, and they aren't meant to be. They twist, turn, ascend, and descend, creating a mosaic of experiences that shape who we are.

Uncertainty, while challenging, is manageable. It's a testament to the infinite possibilities that life offers. Overcoming it involves introspection, action, resilience, and the knowledge that seeking help is okay. Remember, the darkest nights often precede the most beautiful dawns. Embrace the journey, for it's in traversing through the valleys of uncertainty that we often find our most authentic selves and the most rewarding experiences.

Embracing New Responsibilities and Independence

Milestones punctuate the adventure of life, each carrying its weight and wonder. Among the most significant are the dawn of independence and the responsibilities it ushers in. This phase is a rite of passage, a beautiful contrast of freedom and accountability that heralds the transition into full-fledged adulthood. It's a season of growth, discovery, and empowerment, and while it can sometimes feel overwhelming, it's, in truth, one of life's most enriching experiences.

The allure of independence is woven into our very fabric from a young age. Remember the first time you tied your shoes, rode a bike without training wheels, or managed to cook a simple dish? These might seem like minor achievements, but they were our initial steps toward autonomy. As we grow older, the canvas of independence expands. Suddenly, it's not just about tying shoelaces but managing finances, maintaining a household, navigating a career, or even starting a family.

With this newfound freedom comes the inevitable counterpart - responsibility. It's our silent agreement with life: "Grant me the freedom to steer my ship, and I'll accept the responsibility for the course it takes." This exchange, while intimidating, is also the crucible in which character is forged and authentic self-awareness is born.

One of the foundational responsibilities that independence brings is self-reliance. This means taking care of our basic needs and ensuring our emotional, mental, and social well-being. It's about understanding that while reaching out for support when needed is essential, the primary responsibility for our happiness, health, and growth rests on our shoulders. This self-reliance is a journey that starts with understanding oneself, recognizing one's strengths and weaknesses, and cultivating a proactive approach to life.

Financial independence is another crucial aspect that most young adults grapple with. The freedom to earn and spend comes with the duty to manage, save, invest, and plan for the future. It's no longer just about immediate gratifications but about making choices that ensure stability and security. This might mean setting budgets, understanding taxes, or even delving into the intricacies of investments and retirement planning.

Then there's the responsibility towards relationships. As young adults, relationships evolve from casual school friendships to bonds that require effort, understanding, and commitment. This could be through romantic relationships, professional networks, or even deepened familial ties. Independence means freedom to choose our tribe, but it also necessitates the maturity to nurture, sustain, and sometimes even end relationships with grace and empathy.

Embracing independence also means understanding the broader responsibilities we hold as citizens and members of society. It's about recognizing that our actions have a ripple effect, no matter how insignificant they may seem. Whether voting in an election, volunteering for a cause or merely being a conscious consumer, independent individuals have important roles to play in society.

While responsibility is a significant part of independence, it's essential to maintain sight of the joy, adventure, and growth it offers. Every challenge faced, and every hurdle overcome, adds a new dimension to our character. The choices we make, the paths we tread, and even the mistakes we make are all essential to the narrative of our lives.

So, how does one strike a balance? How do we embrace the exhilaration of independence without being overwhelmed by its responsibilities? The answer lies in perspective. Like every other phase of life, this journey is a learning experience. There will be moments of clarity and doubt, highs that make you feel invincible, and lows that ground you. And that's okay. The key is approaching it with an open heart, a curious mind, and the resilience to keep moving forward.

Lean into the resources at your disposal. This could be through books, mentors, peers, or even professional advisors in areas where you need more knowledge and confidence. Remember, seeking guidance is not a sign of weakness but of wisdom.

In essence, embracing new responsibilities and independence is a dance. A dance where freedom and responsibility sway in harmony, complementing each other. It's a journey that promises growth, self-awareness, and a deepened appreciation for life. As you stand on this threshold, take a moment to revel in the possibilities, accept the challenges, and embark on this adventure with optimism and determination. In embracing independence, we find not just responsibility, but the true essence of who we are and who we can become.

Chapter 3

In a world where putting on a brave face and showcasing only our best moments has become the norm, exposing our raw, unfiltered emotions and experiences might seem daunting. Yet, in this very act of vulnerability, we unearth our most profound strengths.

Imagine walking through a gallery, each portrait representing a facet of your life. Some paintings depict joyous occasions: graduations, birthdays, and successes. Others, however, unveil challenging moments: heartbreaks, failures, and doubts. These portraits, though less picturesque, are essential. They signify vulnerability and hold stories that resonate deeply, not just with you, but with everyone who views them.

A Shift from the Norm

Society has always encouraged us to be strong and build fortresses around our feelings, ensuring our insecurities and fears remain hidden. But what if we viewed vulnerability not as a weakness but as a bridge that connects us with others, fostering understanding and compassion?

Sarah, a writer by profession, had always struggled with embracing her vulnerabilities. She penned tales about fictional characters, masking her experiences behind a veil of imagination. However, after a heart-wrenching breakup on one fateful evening, she sat down and began pouring her feelings onto paper. The result was a raw, heartfelt narrative about love, loss, and healing.

When she shared this piece with the world, the response was overwhelming. Messages poured in from people across the globe, resonating with her words, sharing their own stories of pain and recovery. Sarah had unwittingly tapped into the universal power of vulnerability.

Unveiling Authenticity

By opening up, Sarah had gifted her readers with authenticity—a real, tangible connection built on shared human experiences. She found that in moments of vulnerability, people aren't looking for a superhero; they seek authenticity. They yearn for someone who understands, who's been there, and who's still navigating the maze of life.

Catalyst for Growth

Vulnerability is more than just sharing our trials; it's about acknowledging and using them as stepping stones. Sarah's heartbreak, which once seemed like a setback, catalyzed personal growth. Embracing her vulnerability helped her process her emotions, understand her desires better, and eventually find a more profound, more genuine connection with herself and others.

Fostering Connections

There's a reason why support groups are influential. They provide a platform for individuals to be vulnerable, to share, and in the process, find solace in the fact that they aren't alone. The power of vulnerability lies in its ability to foster deep, meaningful connections. When we shed our protective layers, we allow others to see us—not as infallible beings, but as humans with flaws, dreams, and emotions. This paves the way for more profound empathy, understanding, and connection.

Breaking the Chains of Perfection

In the age of social media, where life often seems picture-perfect, vulnerability serves as a refreshing reminder of reality. It tells us it's okay not to be okay, that perfection is a myth, and that everyone is fighting their battles, no matter how put-together they seem.

A Journey, Not a Destination

Embracing vulnerability is not a one-time act; it's a continuous journey of self-awareness and growth. It's about regularly checking in with oneself, understanding one's emotions, and not shying away from seeking help when needed. Vulnerability is a commitment to authenticity, even when the world demands otherwise.

Vulnerability, often misconstrued as a sign of weakness, is one of our most potent strengths. It's a testament to our humanity and our capacity to feel, heal, and connect. By embracing our vulnerabilities, we allow ourselves to grow and offer others a mirror to their own experiences, fostering a world of understanding, compassion, and authentic connections. Like Sarah, when we open our hearts and share our stories, we realize that vulnerability is not just about unmasking our true selves but also about discovering the universality of human experiences, struggles, and triumphs.

Overcoming Fear of Judgment

In a quaint town nestled among rolling hills, there once lived a young artist named Clara. Clara painted with her soul's deepest emotions, not with colors and brushes. However, instead of displaying her art, she hid it, fearing what others might think. And while this story is about Clara, it resonates with many of us who've locked away parts of ourselves, terrified of judgment.

The fear of judgment has been our uninvited companion through-out human history. It lurks in the shadows, whispering tales of ridicule and rejection, holding us back from expressing our true selves. But what if we could silence that voice? What if we could walk through life with our heads held high, immune to the imagined whispers and stares?

Clara's journey to overcome her fear of judgment began on a sum-mer day when her niece, Lucy, stumbled upon one of her hidden paintings. It was a haunting portrayal of a lonely figure standing at the crossroads, an embodiment of Clara's internal struggles. Lucy's eyes lit up with wonder. "Aunt Clara, this is beautiful! Why don't you show it to the world?"

Clara hesitated. "What if they don't like it? What if they laugh?"

Lucy, with the innocence of a child, replied, "But I love it. And isn't one genuine compliment worth more than a hundred fake praises?"

Lucy's words struck a chord. That evening, as the golden hues of sunset painted the sky, Clara found herself pondering her fears. Why was she so afraid of judgment? Why did the potential criticism of a few outweigh the possible appreciation of many?

The roots of our fear of judgment often run deep, intertwined with past experiences and societal expectations. Perhaps it's a childhood memory of being mocked or the relentless pursuit of perfection in a constantly scrutinized world. But as Clara realized, it's not the judg-ment itself that's daunting; it's the power we give it.

She remembered an old saying, "People will judge you no matter what you do, so you might as well do what you love." It was time to break free.

Determined to face her fears, Clara displayed her paintings at the local art fair. The night before the event, anxiety gnawed at her. But she remembered Lucy's words and took deep breaths, focusing on the love and passion that went into her art rather than the expected reactions.

The day of the fair was a whirlwind. As people passed by her stall, Clara saw various reactions. Some glanced and moved on, a few stopped to critique, but many stood captivated, lost in the emotions her paintings evoked.

An older man, his face etched with lines of age and wisdom, stood silently before the painting of the lonely figure at the crossroads. Tears glistened in his eyes. He turned to Clara, "This... this speaks to me. It reminds me of a time when I stood at my crossroads, uncertain and alone. Thank you for creating this."

That moment was transformative for Clara. The fear of judgment, which had once loomed like an insurmountable mountain, had diminished. She realized that by embracing authenticity, she had touched lives.

Of course, there were criticisms and unkind remarks. But they paled in comparison to the genuine connections and appreciation. Clara learned judgments are fleeting, but the impact of authenticity is everlasting.

Clara's art gained recognition as days turned into weeks and weeks into months. Not because it catered to everyone, but because it was genuine. It was a reflection of her soul, her struggles, and her triumphs. And in her journey, she inspired many, teaching them the value of authenticity over conformity.

In our lives, we'll always encounter moments when the fear of judgment threatens to hold us back. But just like Clara, we must remember that it's better to be disliked for being authentic than to be loved for being something we're not.

In the grand scheme of life, it's not the praises or the criticisms that define us, but our courage to be true to ourselves.

As Clara's story illustrates, when we overcome our fear of judgment and embrace our authentic selves, we not only find inner peace but also forge genuine connections, touch lives, and leave an indelible mark on the world.

Emotional Intelligence and Authentic Living

There's a powerful story of a young woman named Ava who lived in a bustling metropolis. Every day, she wore a mask — not a physical one, but an emotional facade. She would smile, even if her heart was heavy, laugh when she felt like crying, and pretend everything was perfect when her world was crumbling. Like many of us, Ava believed showing genuine emotions was a sign of weakness. But her journey into emotional intelligence taught her the profound connection between authentic living and genuinely understanding one's emotions.

As the story goes, Ava worked in a high-pressure corporate job. She was a master at concealing her emotions, ensuring that her colleagues saw her as a strong and calm professional. But this emotional bottling came at a cost. She felt isolated, disconnected from her true self, and deeply unhappy.

One evening, after a stressful day at work, Ava stumbled upon a book about emotional intelligence in a quaint little bookstore. Understanding and managing emotions could lead to a more fulfilled life that intrigued her. She decided to delve deeper.

Emotional intelligence, Ava learned, was not just about identifying and understanding emotions but also about harnessing these emotions for tasks like problem-solving and connecting with others. The skill allows us to navigate our emotional world with finesse.

But here's where Ava had an epiphany: emotional intelligence is deeply tied to authentic living. By understanding her emotions, she could live more authentically. But how?

She began by practicing self-awareness. Instead of pushing her feelings aside, she started acknowledging them. If she felt overwhelmed, she'd step aside, take a few deep breaths, and ask herself, "Why am I feeling this way?" By recognizing her emotions, she began to understand them.

Next, she focused on self-regulation. Instead of reacting impulsively, Ava started responding thoughtfully. When a colleague made a snide remark, instead of snapping back, she'd pause, understand her rising anger, and then choose to react calmly.

Her journey into emotional intelligence also introduced her to the art of empathy. Ava realized that just as she hid her emotions, others did too. She began to pick up on non-verbal cues, understanding what others were feeling, and connecting with them on a deeper level. Instead of offering a standard response to a distressed friend, she'd genuinely listen, empathize, and provide comfort.

But the most transformative aspect of her journey was embracing authenticity. She realized that understanding her emotions was liberating. Instead of wearing a mask, she began to show up as her genuine self. She'd share her fears, joys, and disappointments. She laughed when something was funny and allowed herself to cry when hurt.

The results were profound. Not only did she feel more connected to herself, but her relationships also deepened. People were drawn to her authentic self. Colleagues valued her emotional insight, friends cherished her genuine empathy, and she felt more personally and professionally fulfilled.

One evening, reflecting on her journey, she wrote in her diary, "By understanding my emotions, I've discovered my true self. Emotional intelligence is not just about navigating the world of feelings; it's about living authentically in a world that often encourages us to hide our true selves."

Ava's story resonates with many of us. To fit into societal molds, we often suppress our emotions. But our emotions are the very essence of our being. They provide light on our deepest aspirations, fears, and dreams. By understanding and embracing them, we can live more authentically.

In the tapestry of life, where each thread represents an emotion, emotional intelligence is the skill that allows us to weave a beautiful story. A story where we're not just existing but living. A story where we're not just reacting but responding. A story where we're connecting, not just on a superficial level, but deep, heart-to-heart.

So, remember Ava's story the next time you find yourself suppressing a genuine laugh or holding back tears. Dive deep into the ocean of your emotions, understand them, embrace them, and let them guide you to a life of authenticity.

Chapter 4

Humans possess an unlimited variety of experiences, each lending itself to a unique blend of character.

These experiences are born out of our strengths and passions, which shape our stories and give them vibrancy. But how often do we pause to understand the facets of our personalities? To discover what ignites our spirit and drives our actions? By diving deep into the reservoir of our strengths and passions, we unlock a world of potential and purpose.

In its unpredictable beauty, life often pushes us down paths guided by necessity rather than choice. We find ourselves caught in routines, playing roles, and fulfilling self-imposed and external expectations. However, aligning our actions with our strengths and passions is crucial to living a life that resonates with authenticity and joy.

Strengths are like the sturdy roots of a tree, providing stability and nourishment. They are the inherent abilities and attributes that come naturally to us. These range from soft skills like empathy, leadership, and communication to hard skills like writing, analytical thinking, or artistic endeavors. Our strengths set us apart and make us shine, and tapping into them can transform how we perceive and interact with the world.

On the other hand, our passions are the flames that illuminate our path, the winds that propel our sails. They are the activities, ideas, and pursuits that fill us with enthusiasm and joy. Passions make our hearts race a little faster; our eyes sparkle a little brighter. They are not just hobbies or pastimes; they are deep-seated interests that resonate with the core of our being.

So, how does one go about identifying these strengths and passions?

Begin with introspection. Carve out moments of solitude, away from the din of daily life, to reflect on the moments you felt most alive, most competent. Think back to the compliments you've often received, the tasks you excel at with little effort, or the activities where you lose track of time. These are your clues.

Next, seek external feedback. Sometimes, an outsider's perspective can illuminate attributes we might overlook. Engage in conversations with close friends, family, or colleagues. Ask them about your standout qualities and what activities they've seen you thrive in.

Engaging in varied experiences also offers valuable insights. Often, our strengths and passions lie dormant, waiting to be discovered. By pushing our boundaries, trying out new activities, or learning different skills, we might stumble upon facets of ourselves previously unexplored. It could be a workshop, a class, or a casual meetup group.

Journaling can be another powerful tool in this quest. Patterns emerge by putting our ideas, emotions, and experiences into words. Over time, these scribbles and reflections will merge into a clearer picture of what drives you and where your strengths lie.

As we identify our strengths and passions, it's also essential to understand the interplay between them. Just because you're passionate about something doesn't mean it's your strength and vice versa. However, the intersection of the two is where magic happens. It's where tasks feel effortless, where work feels like play, and where challenges become stepping stones to growth.

It's worth noting that strengths and passions can, and most likely will, evolve. Our experiences, learnings, and circumstances can shift our perspectives and priorities as we go through the journey of life. What once ignited us might no longer hold the same allure and strengths once taken for granted and might need refining. And that's okay. The essence lies in staying attuned to these shifts and realigning our paths accordingly.

Embracing our strengths and passions doesn't just elevate our personal and professional lives; it also has a broader impact. When individuals operate from a place of authenticity and enthusiasm, it ripples out, creating more positive, inspired, and vibrant communities. It encourages others to embark on similar journeys of discovery, fostering mutual growth and support.

Identifying our strengths and passions isn't just an exercise in self-awareness; it's a wake-up call to our most authentic selves. It's a journey that promises fulfillment, purpose, and a deeper connection to the fiber of our being. So, as you experience the journey of self-exploration, remember that every step towards understanding and embracing your unique strengths and passions is a step towards a more enriched, empowered, and authentic life.

Different Career Paths

More than just a collection of jobs, a career can be a journey that intertwines our passions, strengths, and life's countless experiences. We embark on this voyage with hopes and dreams, often fueled by youthful idealism. But as we tread forward, the world opens up, revealing a vast spectrum of professions, industries, and opportunities that we may never have considered.

Traditionally, career paths were linear. One chose a field, studied it, and then continued to work in that area for most of their professional life. However, with its ever-evolving technologies, industries, and global interconnectedness, the modern world has drastically expanded its horizons. Today, the career landscape is full of new possibilities, and choosing a path can be both exciting and daunting.

To navigate this vast terrain, we must first dispel the myth of the 'perfect' career. There's no one-size-fits-all solution. Each person's ideal career path uniquely blends their interests, skills, values, and circumstances. Finding the right career is a personal experience, filled with introspection, exploration, and continuous learning.

One of the foundational steps in exploring different career paths is understanding oneself. This involves delving into what excites you, what you're naturally good at, and what aligns with your life's goals and values. Reflect on past experiences, both in academic and extracurricular settings. Which subjects or activities drew you in? When did you feel most accomplished? These memories and feelings can be strong indicators of potential career inclinations.

Simultaneously, arm yourself with knowledge about the multitude of professions out there. Consider attending career fairs, seminars, and workshops. These platforms offer a window into various industries, allowing you to gauge which resonates with you. Engage in conversations with professionals from fields that intrigue you. Their insights, experiences, and advice can provide valuable perspectives often unavailable in books or online resources.

However, knowledge alone is not enough. Immersive learning is critical. Whenever possible, plunge yourself into internships, part-time jobs, or even volunteer work related to your profession of interest. Such firsthand experiences offer a taste of the job and help build networks, acquire new skills, and understand the real-world nuances of a particular career.

In this age of information, online platforms also play a pivotal role. Websites like LinkedIn, online courses, and industry-specific forums can provide valuable insights. They provide a glimpse into the day-to-day workings of various professions, the challenges faced, and the skills required. Many professionals are willing to mentor or guide curious individuals. Reaching out for informational interviews can be a goldmine for those who need guidance with their direction.

While exploring, it's also essential to remain open-minded. The rate of global change is accelerating. Jobs in demand today might be obsolete in a decade, and new, unheard-of professions are cropping up regularly. Staying adaptable, continuously updating skills, and being willing to pivot when necessary are crucial attributes in the modern career landscape.

Additionally, remember that a career is not just about financial stability or social status. It's about personal fulfillment, growth, and contributing to your unique character. Monetary benefits, while essential, are just one aspect. Does the job align with your values? Does it offer opportunities for growth and learning? Will it allow a work-life balance? These are all vital questions to consider.

Exploring different career paths is not a sprint but a marathon. It's a process of trial and error, of learning and evolving. There might be times of doubt, moments where you might feel lost or overwhelmed by the sheer number of choices. In such moments, seeking guidance can be invaluable. Career counselors, mentors, or trusted friends and family can offer clarity, support, and direction.

The realm of careers is vast, dynamic, and full of potential. Each path tells a story, offers challenges, and presents opportunities. As you stand at the crossroads, remember that you're not just choosing a job but crafting a narrative that encompasses your passions, dreams, and the legacy you wish to leave behind. Dive deep, explore with an open heart, and accept the voyage with all its detours. After all, these diverse experiences, choices, and learnings will culminate in a successful and deeply fulfilling career.

Setting Up for Professional Success

Pursuing professional success is similar to preparing for a long, rewarding expedition. One doesn't merely stumble upon success; it's the result of meticulous planning, persistent efforts, and the willingness to adapt and remain flexible. The narrative of thriving professionally is about more than just clinching deals, earning promotions, or reaching the peak of one's industry. It's about crafting a journey with learning, growth, and meaningful contributions.

Each brushstroke matters on the canvas of professional life, from the initial choices and efforts to the continued persistence in the face of adversity. Here's how to set the stage and walk toward lasting professional success.

The Foundation: Self-Awareness and Clarity

At the outset, understanding oneself is paramount. Dive deep into your strengths, weaknesses, passions, and values. This introspection acts as a compass, guiding your decisions and aligning your professional journey with personal fulfillment. Knowing what you bring to the table, what ignites your spirit, and what you stand for makes navigating the intricacies of the professional world easier.

Knowledge and Skills: Lifelong Learning

The world is in constantly changing, and staying updated is no longer a luxury but a necessity. Invest in continuous learning. Whether gaining a new skill, refreshing existing knowledge, or diving into something new, the quest for knowledge ensures you remain relevant and competitive. Workshops, online courses, seminars, or informal discussions can be gold mines of information and perspectives.

Networking: Building Authentic Relationships

Success is not an isolated journey. The relationships you cultivate play an instrumental role in shaping your professional trajectory. But networking isn't just about collecting business cards; it's about building genuine connections. Attend industry events, join professional groups, and actively participate in discussions. Remember, it's the quality of these connections, not the quantity, that can open doors to opportunities and insights.

Mentorship: Guided Navigation

In the vast ocean of professional endeavors, mentors act as lighthouses, guiding you away from potential pitfalls and towards promising shores. Whether it's someone within your organization or an external expert, having a mentor provides a unique blend of encouragement, feedback, and experience-driven advice.

Resilience and Adaptability: The Dynamic Duo

The path to success is often dotted with hurdles and unexpected turns. Resilience is the force that keeps you moving forward, even when the going gets tough. Grit helps you bounce back from failures, learn from mistakes, and turn challenges into stepping stones. Hand in hand with resilience is adaptability—the ability to pivot when required, embrace change, and evolve with the industry's shifting landscapes.

Setting Clear Goals: Chart the course

Envision where you aspire to be in the next year, five years, or even a decade. Setting clear, achievable goals acts as milestones on your journey, giving direction and purpose to your efforts. These aren't just about the significant achievements, but can also encompass personal development, skill acquisition, and other facets that contribute to holistic professional growth.

Work-Life Balance: The Delicate Scale

While professional growth is vital, striking a balance is equally crucial. All work and no play can lead to burnout, diminishing the quality of life and work performance. Create time for relaxation, hobbies, family, and self-care. Remember, a refreshed mind is more productive and creative.

Ethical Grounding: Success with Integrity

In the race to the top, cutting corners can sometimes become tempting. However, lasting success is built on the bedrock of integrity. Making ethically sound decisions earns respect from peers and superiors and ensures you can look back at your journey with pride.

Feedback: The Mirror to Growth

Regularly seek feedback on your performance, initiatives, and ideas. Whether it's from colleagues, superiors, or subordinates, constructive feedback provides fresh perspectives, highlights areas of improvement, and reaffirms strengths.

Celebrate Small Wins: Fueling Motivation

While the endgame might be a significant achievement, it's essential to acknowledge and celebrate the minor victories along the way. These are motivation boosters, reminding you of progress and fueling the drive for future endeavors.

Setting up for professional success is a multifaceted journey, an art that blends personal attributes with external efforts. It's about creating a collage of experiences, learnings, and relationships that propel you toward your goals and enrich the essence of the professional expedition. As you embark on this quest, remember that attaining success is a process rather than a destination.

Chapter 5

The airplane wheels skidded on the runway, sending a rush of excitement through Anna's veins. As she stepped out into the bustling streets of Marrakech, the vibrant hues of the bazaar, the aroma of roasting spices, and the Arabic language were a world away from her usual city life in Chicago. It wasn't just the start of a vacation; it was the beginning of an intricate dance of self-discovery.

Traveling is often perceived as a break from the monotony of daily life–a chance to relax on sandy beaches or capture Instagram-worthy snapshots. But beneath these surface-level experiences lies a profound avenue for personal growth that can transform our perception of the world and our own uniqueness.

The Theater of Unfamiliarity: When we're plucked from the familiar cocoon of our hometowns and planted in a new environment, the world seems both bewildering and captivating. Every interaction, from bartering in a local market to deciphering a foreign menu, becomes a lesson. We become students of life, learning from experiences that textbooks and documentaries cannot provide. This unfamiliarity is not an obstacle but a stage where we confront our adaptability, patience, and resilience.

Challenging Stereotypes: Travel has a beautiful way of debunking myths. What we believe about the big world out there, based on second-hand accounts or media portrayals, is often a skewed version of reality. We grow by immersing ourselves in different cultures, tasting unfamiliar cuisines, and engaging in local customs. We unlearn biases, acknowledge the vastness of human experience, and cultivate a more inclusive and compassionate outlook.

Finding Solitude Amongst the Crowd: Even while being surrounded by busy streets and buzzing landmarks, travel can bring a unique solitude. Anna found hers atop a dune in the Sahara Desert, surrounded by an endless expanse of golden sand, where silence had its own sound. Such moments, far from the digital distractions of modern life, offer deep introspection. They allow us to pause, reflect on our life choices, and reconnect with our inner selves.

The Tapestry of Human Connection: Perhaps the most profound growth comes from the bonds we forge on our journeys. The shared laughter with a group of locals over a failed attempt at a traditional dance, the stories exchanged with a fellow traveler on a night train, or the fleeting yet deep connection with a stranger during a festival reminds us of our shared humanity. We're reminded that the core human emotions—love, joy, hope, and aspirations—are universal despite linguistic, cultural, or geographical barriers.

Resilience in Adversity: Not all travels are smooth. Lost passports, missed connections, or unexpected sickness can turn a dream trip into a nightmare. But these adversities, as challenging as they are, teach us about our inner strength. They instill a problem-solving spirit, leading us to stay calm in crises and find innovative solutions. When Anna lost her baggage during a connecting flight, resourcefulness replaced the initial despair as she navigated the situation. Such experiences provide stories to tell and strengthen our confidence in facing life's many unpredictable challenges.

Expanded Worldview: Traveling makes abstract concepts concrete. Reading about the tranquility of Buddhist monasteries is one thing; witnessing monks in deep meditation amidst the Himalayan peaks is another. These real-life experiences challenge our pre-existing beliefs and offer a broader perspective on life. They make us more informed, open-minded individuals who can appreciate the richness and diversity of global cultures.

Personal Evolution: Each journey changes us. We return not just with souvenirs and photographs but with evolved personalities. The challenges faced, the beauty witnessed, and the connections made leave an indelible mark on our souls. We become more aware, more grateful, and more alive to life's myriad possibilities.

As Anna boarded her flight back, she realized Marrakech had gifted her more than just memories. It had given her insights into her strengths and weaknesses, broadened her worldview, and added layers to her personality. And that's the magic of travel. It's more than just a change of geography; it's a transformative journey of the soul.

So, the next time you pack your bags, remember that each trip is an opportunity for personal evolution. Travel with an open heart and a curious mind. Let the world be your teacher and every experience a lesson. For in the grand odyssey of life, the journey is as significant, if not more, than the destination.

Respecting and Embracing Different Cultures

Juliana stood, transfixed, at the heart of a bustling Tokyo intersection. The organized chaos around her was a symphony of colors, sounds, and movements, starkly contrasting the quaint Italian town she hailed from. As the lights changed and people moved, she found herself amidst a sea of people, bowing courteously at acquaintances and strangers alike. At this moment, surrounded by a culture so different from her own, she realized the profound importance of not just observing but truly understanding and embracing cultural differences.

In today's globalized world, we are closer than ever. Physical borders seem to diminish, but cultural nuances remain strong, forming the backbone of societies.

The fabric of every culture is formed by a multitude of components, such as its past experiences, location, religion, and more, all stitched together through the course of history. To respect and embrace these differences is not just an exercise in tolerance, but a journey into the depths of human civilization and understanding.

Juliana's days in Tokyo were an enlightening revelation. As she navigated the streets, she noticed the subtlest of cultural markers. The meticulous care of bonsai trees is evident in the way shopkeepers greeted customers, the intricate etiquette of a traditional tea ceremony, and the profound respect for nature. While these practices were unfamiliar, she didn't view them as exotic spectacles but as chapters in the grand Japanese narrative, each offering insights into the nation's collective psyche.

But how does one truly embrace and respect another culture?

Juliana's quest for understanding took her to a traditional ryokan, a Japanese inn. She was introduced to "Omotenashi," the Japanese spirit of wholehearted hospitality. The innkeeper, Mrs. Saito, didn't just provide a room; she offered an experience. Every detail was steeped in tradition, from the yukata (casual summer kimono) supplied for guests to the meticulously prepared kaiseki (multi-course meal). As Juliana delved deeper, Mrs. Saito shared stories of each practice, enriching the young traveler's understanding.

Such immersive experiences are the key to genuinely respecting different cultures. It's not enough to be a passive observer. One must engage, ask questions, and, most importantly, listen. No matter how perplexing it may seem, every cultural practice has a story, a reason rooted in history or tradition. By understanding these stories, we move beyond mere acceptance to genuine appreciation.

However, embracing another culture doesn't mean sidelining our own. Juliana found herself sharing tales of Italian traditions with Mrs. Saito. The vibrant festivals, the importance of family, and the passion for food. They discovered the universality of specific human experiences in these shared moments, transcending cultural boundaries. Such exchanges enrich both parties, fostering mutual respect and admiration.

Yet, it's crucial to avoid the trap of cultural appropriation, where one adopts elements of another culture superficially without understanding or respect. Wearing a kimono for a fashion statement vastly differs from donning one in a traditional setting, understanding its significance. The former is materialist, while the latter embraces cultural depth.

Embracing different cultures also broadens our cognitive horizons. It fosters creativity and adaptability and equips us with varied problem-solving tools. By understanding different ways of life, we become more informed and empathetic, capable of navigating the global stage with ease and grace.

As Juliana's Japan vacation ended, she realized she was taking back more than souvenirs. She was returning with stories, experiences, and a newfound respect for a vastly different culture. The world seemed more prominent and smaller—vast in its cultural riches but closely knit in the shared human experience.

When we consider the vast scope of human history, each culture is a unique and vibrant strand that adds texture, vibrancy, and beauty to the whole tapestry. By respecting and embracing these threads, we celebrate diversity and fortify the customs, ensuring they remain vivid and robust for future generations.

Traveling on a Budget

The sun dipped low on the horizon, casting a golden glow on the white-washed buildings of Santorini. Alicia sat on a rustic wooden bench, a glass of local wine in hand, watching the world transform into hues of pink and orange. The best part? This view, this experience, didn't burn a hole in her pocket. She was discovering the world's secrets, one budget decision at a time.

In an era where social media is bursting with images of luxury resorts, first-class flights, and exotic locales, it's easy to assume that travel is a privilege of the wealthy. However, with ingenuity, research, and flexibility, the world's wonders can be accessible to anyone, irrespective of their perceived financial limitations.

For Alicia, her dream of exploring Greece started with diligent planning months in advance. Flight tickets are often the most significant expense, but she knew that booking well in advance and being flexible with travel dates could lead to substantial savings. Utilizing fare comparison sites and setting up price alerts, she snagged a deal that was almost half the usual cost. The key was avoiding peak seasons and being open to traveling during odd hours or taking flights with extended layovers.

Accommodation is the next primary concern for many travelers. At the same time, luxury hotels offer unparalleled comfort but come with hefty price tags. Instead, Alicia turned to local guesthouses, hostels, and platforms that offer couch surfing. Not only was she able to save considerably, but she also enjoyed a more authentic experience, interacting with locals and fellow travelers, sharing stories using a translation app, and gaining insights that no hotel suite could offer.

Food, an essential part of any travel experience, can be enjoyed without splurging on high-end restaurants every night. Alicia quickly learned the joys of street food, local markets, and small family-owned eateries tucked away in alleys. These places commonly offer the most authentic and outstanding cuisine at a small percentage of the cost of more commercial establishments. Plus, they provide an opportunity to interact with locals, understand their culinary traditions, and even pick up a recipe or two!

Getting around was another area where Alicia made intelligent choices. Instead of always relying on taxis or tourist-centric modes, she embraced public transportation. Buses, trams, and trains offer a slice of local life and are incredibly economical. In cities, walking became her favorite mode of transport. It allowed her to discover hidden gems, from quaint cafes to artisanal shops, that she would've missed otherwise.

Traveling on a budget doesn't mean missing out on experiences. Many cities offer free walking tours, where knowledgeable locals guide visitors around significant attractions, sharing stories and facts that bring the place to life. Museums often have days when entry is free or discounted. Natural wonders, from beaches to mountains, come without a price tag. By researching in advance and making informed choices, one can enjoy a rich travel experience without breaking the bank.

But beyond all the practical tips and tricks, traveling on a budget teaches invaluable life lessons. It fosters creativity as one learns to think outside the box, finding alternatives, and hacks. It promotes adaptability, where plans might change based on unforeseen expenses or opportunities. Most importantly, it instills a sense of gratitude and mindfulness. Every experience and every interaction becomes precious as the traveler learns to savor moments without the trappings of luxury.

As the sun finally set on Santorini, Alicia reflected on her journey. She had tasted the local cuisine, interacted with residents, and discovered hidden nooks and crannies of the island, all while sticking to her budget. The satisfaction derived from such a trip was unparalleled.

In the end, travel is less about luxury and more about experiences. It's about immersing oneself in a new culture, understanding different ways of life, and creating memories that last a lifetime. And all of this doesn't require deep pockets, just a passion for discovery and the will to venture beyond constraints.

Chapter 6

Before technology took over our lives, receiving a handwritten letter was the highlight of one's week. Pictures were tangible memories you held in your hands.

Along came the seismic shift that altered the very fabric of human interaction: the dawn of social media. Platforms emerged, beckoning us with the promise of perpetual connection, turning the vast world into a close-knit digital village. But just like any transformative force, social media has bright spots and shadows, making it a double-edged sword.

Imagine, if you will, a vast digital ocean. Floating atop this ocean are ships representing Facebook, Instagram, Twitter, TikTok, and countless other social media platforms. Each ship invites you aboard with the promise of adventures, interactions, and discoveries. Once aboard, you're greeted with a kaleidoscope of colors, sounds, and sights: old friends reconnecting, influencers showcasing their picture-perfect lives, activists rallying for a cause, and artists sharing their creations.

This is the side of social media that dazzles and enchants. It demolishes geographical barriers, allowing a teenager in Tokyo to become best friends with someone from Toronto. These digital communities give voices to the voiceless, enabling them to share their stories, rally for change, and find solace in people who can relate to their struggles.

Businesses flourish as they find audiences beyond borders. Learning becomes a global endeavor as knowledge flows seamlessly from one corner of the world to another.

Yet, as you stand on the deck of this ship, if you look closely, you'll notice that not everything is as rosy as it seems. Alongside the beauty, there's also a storm brewing, characterized by the darker aspects of these platforms.

The lines between reality and virtual reality are often blurred in this vast sea of content. Filtered photographs and curated lives can set unrealistic beauty standards, success, and happiness. The constant barrage of these images can leave individuals, especially impressionable young minds, grappling with self-worth and identity issues. They wonder, "Why doesn't my life look as perfect as theirs?"

Further into the depths of this ocean are the treacherous waters of cyberbullying and online harassment. Behind the veil of anonymity, individuals often unleash their worst selves, leaving scars on the psyches of their targets. In such a world, every comment, like, or share, can become a measure of one's self-worth, leading to a relentless pursuit of validation.

The constant need to stay updated, and to be in the loop, can tether us to our devices. "Fear of missing out" (FOMO) develops into a persistent hum in the background, leading to stress, anxiety, and a decreased ability to be present in the real world.

But social media's most subtle and insidious danger is its potential to create echo chambers. Algorithms are designed to show us what we like, leading us to consume content that aligns with our beliefs. Over time, this can cause a narrow worldview, polarizing societies, and fostering intolerance.

So, how does one navigate this tumultuous sea, embracing the positives while steering clear of the negatives?

Mindfulness is the compass that can guide us. It's vital to be aware of why we use social media, recognizing when it uplifts us and when it drains us. If scrolling through your feed makes you feel inadequate or anxious, it might be time to reassess whom you follow or even take a digital detox.

Setting boundaries is equally crucial. Allocate specific times for social media, ensuring it doesn't infringe upon moments dedicated to family, self-care, or simply being present in the real world.

While creating a highlight reel of our lives is tempting, being authentic can be liberating. It fosters genuine connections and breaks the cycle of perpetuating unrealistic standards.

Remember that behind every profile is a human with emotions, struggles, and stories. Practicing kindness, empathy, and understanding can make the digital realm a more compassionate space for all.

Social media has many aspects, just like fire. It can warm us, enlighten us, and bring us together. But unchecked, it can also burn and consume us. The key lies in harnessing its power mindfully, ensuring that, in this digital age, we remain anchored to the timeless values of empathy, authenticity, and human connection.

Setting Boundaries and Digital Detox

In the fast-paced digital age, our lives revolve around screens. From waking up to the trill of an alarm on our smartphones to winding down with a late-night scroll on our favorite social media app, the glow of screens envelops us. But as much as technology has expanded our horizons, it's equally essential to understand the need for boundaries and the refreshing realm of a digital detox.

Imagine for a moment the comforting hum of a coffee shop. Picture yourself there, savoring a latte with a book cradled in your hands. The scene is serene and timeless. Now, superimpose upon this image the blinding glare of screens. Everywhere you look, people are engrossed in their devices, the atmosphere punctuated by the click of keyboards and notification chimes. The contrast is jarring, a stark reminder of how profoundly technology has permeated our existence.

There's no denying the many benefits of this digital era. Virtual meetings have obliterated the constraints of geography, information is at our fingertips, and social media bridges the gap between long-lost friends and families. But there's a flip side to this coin: the constant bombardment of notifications, the compulsion to document every life event, and the unending pressure to stay "updated." Our minds, forever buzzing with digital stimuli, rarely get a moment of respite.

Over time, this dependency and overexposure can manifest in various ways. Our sleep patterns might be disrupted, with the blue light from screens tricking our brains into wakefulness. Our posture can suffer, our eyes get strained, and our mental health can dwindle. We might feel increasingly anxious or depressed, finding it challenging to disconnect from the virtual world and engage with the tangible, beautiful world around us.

And so, setting boundaries and indulging in a digital detox isn't merely a luxury; it's a necessity. It's the conscious decision to reclaim our time, mental peace, and connection with the world beyond pixels.

Setting boundaries doesn't have to be a radical act. Boundaries start with small steps. It could be as simple as designating "no-screen" times during the day, perhaps during meals or the last hour before sleep. It's about cultivating mindfulness. Recognizing moments when reaching for our device is a reflex rather than a necessity. Why are we checking our phones? Is it out of habit? Boredom? Or is there a genuine need?

It's also crucial to establish technology-free spaces. Bedrooms, for example, can be sanctuaries for rest, empty of the demands of emails or the intrigue of social media. When spending time with loved ones, dedicating oneself entirely to the conversation, without the interruption of screens, we can forge more profound, meaningful connections.

Beyond daily boundaries, there's the transformative experience of a digital detox — a more extended period where one consciously disconnects from the digital world. It could be a weekend getaway, spending time in nature, a meditation retreat, or a day spent indulging in hobbies and activities that rejuvenate the soul. The joy of painting, reading a physical book, the thrill of hiking — there are many experiences waiting to be embraced, away from the glow of screens.

During a digital detox, the initial hours might be challenging. The phantom vibration syndrome might kick in, where you feel your phone vibrate even when it hasn't. The compulsion to check emails or social media might be overwhelming. But as the hours morph into days, a remarkable transformation occurs. The world seems more vibrant, sounds become more profound, and the mind, unburdened from the shackles of constant connectivity, flourishes with its newfound freedom.

While the digital realm offers unparalleled advantages, it's vital to tread with awareness and intention. By setting boundaries and allowing ourselves the gift of a digital detox, we're not shunning technology. Instead, we're establishing a harmonious relationship with it, ensuring that we harness its benefits without letting it overshadow the wild wonders of the world around us. The key to a life of contentment, mindfulness, and genuine connection lies in this delicate balance.

Mindful Consumption and Authentic Expression Online

The internet is a vast sea of information, conversations, and experiences. It's an expansive digital landscape that intertwines our lives, stories, and identities. The lines between reality and the virtual world can blur as we navigate this intricate web. It becomes easy to consume content mindlessly and to project idealized versions of ourselves. But, as with all tools, the key to using the internet productively lies in mindful consumption and authentic expression.

Imagine strolling through a massive library with infinite aisles and shelves stretching beyond the horizon, each book more colorful and enticing than the last. The internet is that endless library. Every click, swipe, or tap opens a new chapter, a fresh narrative. But the vastness, while exhilarating, can also be overwhelming. Faced with endless choices, we can sometimes find ourselves drifting aimlessly. We waste valuable time on content that doesn't truly enrich or entertain us. Or worse, we come away feeling inadequate, anxious, or disappointed, comparing our lives to the polished, picture-perfect snapshots we see online.

Mindful consumption is about navigating this vast digital library with intention and purpose. It's about curating a meaningful online experience. Ask yourself, what do you seek from the internet? Is it knowledge, entertainment, connection, inspiration, or a mix? Once you identify your purpose, you can tailor your online journey to align with it. Subscribe to channels or follow accounts that resonate with your goals. The same way you would choose which books to read in a vast library—selecting those that pique your interest and contribute to your growth.

Be aware of the amount of time you spend online. Periodic checks on screen time or using apps that limit your daily social media usage can be eye-opening. They allow you to reclaim your time, redirecting those hours to pursuits that nourish your soul and mind. Read a book, practice an instrument, cook a new recipe, or take a walk. Sometimes, the offline world holds treasures that the digital realm can't match.

Now, let's turn the lens to self-expression. The internet isn't just a space for consumption; it's a platform where we share our stories, ideas, and identities. But there's a trap here—a pressure to portray a version of ourselves that aligns with trending norms or ideals. This pressure can be subtle. It might manifest in the choice of a filter for a photo, the crafting of a caption, or the hesitation before sharing an opinion.

Authentic expression is about breaking free from these invisible chains. It's about recognizing and valuing the uniqueness of your journey, voice, and perspective. Every individual is a who they are because of unique experiences, beliefs, and dreams. When we mute our authentic voice to fit a mold, the world retains the richness and diversity of genuine narratives.

However, authentic expression doesn't mean baring your soul at all times or sharing every facet of your life. It's about being true to yourself in what you choose and how you share it. Celebrate your achievements, but don't shy away from discussing failures. They're two sides of the same coin, shaping the individual you become. Share moments of joy, but also allow yourself to be vulnerable enough to discuss challenges, fears, and uncertainties.

This authenticity fosters deeper connections. When you're genuine online, you attract a community that resonates with your values and experiences. These connections can be profoundly beneficial by providing support, understanding, and diverse perspectives that broaden your horizons.

The internet mirrors life with its vastness and depth. Some paths lead to knowledge, avenues that entertain, and corners that foster connections. As we navigate this space, the compasses of mindful consumption and authentic expression can guide us. They ensure that our digital journey is about passing the time and enriching our lives. In this intentional journey, we don't just consume content; we engage with it. And we don't just project an image; we share our authentic selves. It's a dance of give and take, where we imbibe the best of the digital world while contributing our unique notes to the ever-evolving symphony of the internet.

Chapter 7

Lucy stood on the threshold of her new apartment, keys jingling in her hand, the weight of adulthood upon her shoulders. Moving away from the security of her childhood home, she was confronted with rent, utilities, groceries, and the myriad of bills accompanying independent living. The realization was crystal clear: she had to be meticulous about her finances to thrive in this new chapter of life. Thus, her journey into the world of budgeting and saving began.

Lucy, like many, needed clarification about budgeting. She thought it would mean depriving herself of minor pleasures or only those on a tight income required it. But soon, she discovered that budgeting was a lens, a perspective to view her income and expenditures, allowing her to make informed decisions.

Her first paycheck came, and the euphoria of having her own money was overwhelming. But she remembered her grandmother's advice: "It's not about how much you earn, but how wisely you spend." With this wisdom in her heart, Lucy decided to allocate her money purposefully.

Her primary strategy involved understanding her inflows and outflows. She began by noting down her fixed monthly income. Then, she accounted for her fixed costs: the rent, monthly subscriptions, and utilities. These were non-negotiables and had to be prioritized. Next came the variable expenses, which would differ in monthly activities, including eating out, entertainment, or shopping.

As Lucy navigated this newfound terrain, she realized that creating a budget didn't mean living frugally; it meant living mindfully. It allowed her to indulge occasionally, but in a way that didn't hamper her long-term financial goals.

One afternoon, over a homemade sandwich and a magazine on financial wellness, Lucy stumbled upon the concept of an 'Emergency Fund.' The idea was simple but profound. No matter how well one plans, life is unpredictable. This fund acted as a financial cushion for unplanned events, be it a medical emergency or sudden job loss. It wasn't long before Lucy started setting aside a tiny percentage of her income towards this.

Then there was the 'Savings Bucket.' This wasn't just about stashing money away. It was a representation of her dreams: a solo travel expedition, a course in photography, or even a future down payment for a house. Every month, a particular portion of her salary entered this bucket.

With her budgeting strategy in place, Lucy felt empowered. She was no longer at the mercy of unforeseen expenses or impulsive purchases. She was in control. However, she also recognized the importance of adaptability. If she splurged a little on her birthday month, she'd compensate by being slightly more frugal the next.

But budgeting wasn't just about today; it was about securing tomorrow. Lucy began educating herself about essential investment opportunities. Stock, bond, and mutual fund markets were initially daunting, but with each article she read and seminar she attended, it became more manageable.

To help her along the journey, Lucy opted for a mix of traditional and modern tools. She maintained a ledger, a nod to her grandfather's age-old practices. But she also embraced technology, using budgeting apps that provided analytics, reminders, and insights to refine her financial strategies.

Months rolled by, and Lucy's discipline bore fruit. She had enough for her emergency fund, her savings were growing steadily, and she even dabbled in investing, watching her money grow. The joy of seeing her financial dreams manifest was unparalleled.

One evening, sipping her tea, Lucy reflected on her journey. Budgeting and saving had transformed her life. It was more than just numbers; it was about freedom, security, and empowerment. It was about making choices today that her future self would be thankful for.

In this modern age, where the allure of consumerism is robust and instant gratification is often sought, budgeting is a beacon. It serves as a gentle reminder of our dreams, goals, and the future we aspire to build. Lucy's story shows that budgeting isn't about constraining oneself but paving a path to holistic financial wellness.

Lucy's tale is an inspiration for all venturing into personal finance. Embracing budgeting and saving isn't a chore, but a transformative journey. As you enter this world, remember Lucy's insights, challenges, and successes. They stand testament to the idea that with intention, discipline, and a clear vision, financial freedom is attainable for everyone.

Understanding Debt and How to Manage It

We live in a world where debt has almost become a rite of passage. From student loans to mortgages, credit cards to personal loans, the red digits in our balance sheets often outnumber the black. But is all debt bad? How does one navigate this minefield of borrowing and emerge unscathed? Let's dive deep into understanding debt and charting how to manage it effectively.

Imagine for a moment a ship caught in a storm. For many, debt feels like this overwhelming and seemingly never-ending storm. But even in the fiercest storm, with the right navigation tools, a ship can find its way to calm waters. Debt management is this navigation.

The first step in any journey is understanding where you are. To indeed manage your debt, you must first know it intimately. This is more than just knowing how much you owe. It's about understanding interest rates, payment schedules, penalties, and associated fees. It recognizes the difference between 'good' debt (like mortgages or student loans that potentially add value or increase one's net worth) and 'bad' debt (like high-interest credit cards or payday loans).

Like many of his peers, James was a young professional who found himself entangled in the web of credit cards. The freedom they offered was intoxicating. Little did he realize how quickly minimum payments ballooned with staggering interest rates. But James's turning point came when he sat down one evening, spread out all his statements, and tallied up every cent he owed. The number was daunting, but it was also enlightening. For the first time, he had a clear picture of his debt. He realized that paying the minimum was not even covering the interest. It was a sobering realization and the beginning of his path to freedom.

Now, knowing your debt amount is only half the battle. The next step is to devise a strategy. For some, it's the 'snowball method,' where small debts are cleared first, giving a sense of achievement and motivation to tackle larger ones. The 'avalanche method' works better for others, focusing on high-interest debts first to reduce the overall interest paid over time.

James opted for a hybrid approach. He targeted one high-interest card and aimed to clear a smaller loan, seeking financial prudence and motivational boosts. He consolidated some of his debt, transferring from high-interest cards to lower-interest ones.

Budgeting became James's new mantra. He began tracking his spending, identifying areas where he could cut back. Dining out was reduced, unnecessary subscriptions were canceled, and impulse online shopping became a thing of the past. Every saved penny was redirected to repaying his debt.

But debt management isn't just about cutbacks. It's also about finding new streams of income. James started freelancing on weekends. He sold items he no longer needed. Slowly but surely, his debt started reducing.

During this period, he also sought education. He attended financial seminars, read books on money management, and even sought advice from a financial counselor. This holistic approach helped him repay his debt and understand the behavioral patterns that led to it. He learned the value of an emergency fund, the importance of saving for the future, and, most crucially, living within one's means.

After two years, James managed to clear 80% of his debt. He still uses a credit card today but pays off the entire balance each month, enjoying the benefits without the pitfalls.

Debt, in many ways, is like fire. It can be a helpful tool, providing warmth and light, or it can be destructive, consuming everything in its path. The difference lies in understanding and control.

James's journey from being trapped in debt to achieving financial freedom offers a blueprint. Recognize the full scope of your debt, devise a tailored strategy, be disciplined in your spending, seek additional income, and continuously educate yourself. With these tools, the debt storm can be navigated, leading to the calm waters of financial stability and peace of mind.

Introduction to Investments and Growing Wealth

From the need for shelter and basic necessities to the more aspirational desires like travel and luxury, money is the tool that facilitates our ambitions and dreams. Yet, for many, the narrative around money is one of mere survival, with paychecks evaporating almost as soon as they arrive. But what if there's another story to be told? A story where money is not just spent but is also grown? This is the tale of investments and the art of growing wealth.

Imagine for a moment a tree—a sapling, to be precise, fragile and unassuming. Left alone, it might grow, but its chances are left to the whims of nature. Now, consider that you decide to nurture it. You water it, shield it from harsh conditions, and ensure it has the nutrients it needs. Given time, this sapling transforms into a towering tree, robust and fruitful. This is the essence of investment - taking what's small, nurturing it, and watching it flourish.

At its core, investing is about laying down money today with the expectation of having more money in the future. It's a promise of growth, a commitment to the idea that your financial resources can be channeled so that they multiply. However, much like our tree analogy, investments require care, understanding, and patience.

The world of investing is as varied as it is vast. From the stock market, where shares of companies are bought and sold, to real estate, where property becomes the asset of focus, the avenues are diverse. There are bonds, where you lend money to entities like governments or corporations, or mutual funds, where professionals manage a pool of funds from various investors. And in recent times, the digital age has ushered in the era of cryptocurrencies, adding another layer to the investment cake.

So, where does one begin?

The journey starts with self-awareness. Understand your risk appetite. Can you ride the highs and lows of the stock market, or does the mere thought make your stomach churn? Next, consider your financial goals. Are you investing for a comfortable retirement, a child's education, or that dream vacation to the coast of California?

Once you've mapped out your profile, it's time for education. Dive into books, attend online classes, watch related video content, and listen to informative podcasts. Equip yourself with knowledge. While filled with opportunities, the world of investing is also riddled with complexities. There's the enigma of market trends, understanding economic indicators, and diversification strategies. It's a realm where knowledge is not just power but the compass guiding decision-making.

For Alicia, a 28-year-old graphic designer, the investment journey began with a simple savings account. She'd stash away a portion of her paycheck, watching it grow at a modest interest rate. But as she delved deeper into financial literacy, Alicia realized there were richer soils where her money could thrive. She started small, investing in mutual funds, then gradually ventured into stocks, choosing companies she believed in. Over time, with research and some advice from financial experts, her portfolio grew in size and diversity. Today, some of her wealth is even tied up in digital assets, a testament to her evolving investment prowess.

Investing, it's worth noting, is about more than quick wins. It's a marathon, not a sprint. There will be periods where the numbers dip, the economy wavers, and choices don't yield the desired results. But the magic of investing lies in persistence and the unwavering belief that well-chosen assets grow in the long run. It's the power of compound interest, where interest earns interest, and wealth isn't just accumulated; it's multiplied.

As you embark on this journey, remember that investments are tools in the larger scheme of financial well-being. It's about ensuring that as the years roll on, your quality of life remains undiminished and that dreams are envisioned and realized. Investing is about growing wealth, but more importantly, it's about enriching life.

So, as you embark on this exciting voyage, take a moment to envision the future. See the tree in its full glory, branches riddled with fruits, a testament to patience and care. That is the potential of your wealth, waiting to be unlocked and grow. Welcome to the world of investments.

Chapter 8

E very life experience has the ability to mold us, influence us, and even challenge us. From friendships to romances, every relationship we cultivate has the power to either enrich our lives or drain us. Like the water we drink, relationships can be a source of nourishment and growth, or, likewise, they can be toxic and harmful. Knowing how to discern between healthy and unhealthy relationships is beneficial and essential for our well-being.

Imagine you are a gardener. In your garden, you have a variety of plants. Some are vibrant, full of life, and fill your garden with fragrance. Despite your best efforts, others seem to wilt, overshadowing the blossoms nearby. Much like plants, relationships need care, attention, and the right environment to flourish.

A healthy relationship is similar to a radiant flower, grounded with solid roots. Such relationships are built on mutual respect. Both parties understand and value each other's boundaries, acknowledging that they share a bond and are individual entities with unique needs and aspirations. There's a sense of security—a trust that the other person has your back, not because they are obliged to, but because they genuinely care.

Open communication is another hallmark of a healthy relationship. Imagine sharing your thoughts, feelings, fears, and dreams without fear of judgment. It's a safe space where both transparency and vulnerability are celebrated. The arguments or disagreements that arise—and they will, for no relationship is without hiccups—are addressed with maturity. There's an inherent desire to understand, listen, and grow together.

On the other side of the spectrum lies the toxic relationship. It's the plant that, despite all the sunshine, continues to wilt, casting a shadow on its surroundings. Such relationships often have an imbalance of power, where one party feels the need to control or dominate the other. Instead of mutual respect, there's emotional, physical, or psychological manipulation. Walking on eggshells becomes a familiar feeling as unpredictability looms large.

Toxic relationships drain energy. They bring forth feelings of constant anxiety, unhappiness, or inadequacy. Far from being open, communication is either stifled or erupts in volatile outbursts. A persistent undercurrent of negativity makes even good days seem overshadowed.

Recognizing these traits is one thing; understanding their impact on our lives is another. Healthy relationships are like the wind beneath our wings. They empower, motivate, and inspire. They bring out the best in us, pushing us towards growth and self-improvement. There's a shared joy in achievements and a shoulder to lean on during tough times. The happiness and contentment from such relationships often spill over to other areas of our lives, creating a positive feedback loop.

In contrast, toxic relationships are like chains weighing us down. Constant stress and negativity can affect mental health, leading to depression, anxiety, or low self-esteem. Physical fitness, too, can take a hit, as chronic stress is linked to many ailments. What's more, the cloud of a toxic relationship can overshadow other areas of life, impacting work, friendships, and personal growth.

So, what should one do when faced with the realization of being in a toxic relationship? The first step is acknowledgment. Denial is a common defense mechanism, but healing begins with acceptance. Seeking support, be it from friends, family, or professionals, can be invaluable. Remember, it's okay to prioritize your well-being and happiness. Sometimes, the bravest thing one can do is walk away from toxicity, embracing the promise of healthier, happier relationships.

The relationships we nurture profoundly impact our life's journey. By learning to recognize the signs of healthy and toxic relationships, we equip ourselves to make informed choices that resonate with our quest for happiness, growth, and well-being. In the grand garden of life, may your path be adorned with blossoms of love, respect, and mutual growth.

Building and Maintaining Trust

In the vast ocean of human emotions and connections, trust is the anchor that holds our ships steady. Trust ensures we don't drift away amidst the currents of misunderstandings, misgivings, and misfortunes. It's a foundational aspect of any relationship—a bond that acts as a glue, joining two souls together. Without it, our interpersonal ties are as fleeting as sandcastles, beautiful to look at but unable to withstand the test of time and tide.

Imagine, for a moment, a bridge. This bridge represents trust, linking two shores or people together. To cross this bridge and reach the other side, one must have complete confidence in its stability. A missing plank or a tiny crack can cause hesitation, fear, or even a refusal to cross. Similarly, trust in relationships serves as this bridge. Trust connects our hearts and ensures that the emotional and psychological bond remains intact even when we're apart.

The journey to building such an invulnerable bridge of trust is no small feat. It's not a monument erected overnight or built with flimsy materials made up of shallow promises and fleeting emotions. It's crafted with the bricks of consistency, the cement of authenticity, and the pillars of mutual respect.

Trust takes root in the soil of reliability at the beginning of any relationship, whether romantic, platonic, or professional. Every kept promise, every small act of showing up when it matters, and every gesture that resonates with authenticity lays the foundation. It's like the first handshake, firm and reassuring, promising the start of something genuine.

As trust deepens, it ushers in a new realm: vulnerability. To truly trust someone is to let down one's guard, to open up the hidden recesses of our souls, revealing our fears, hopes, dreams, and scars. It's to share one's story, confident that the listener will neither mock nor misuse this sacred knowledge. In these profound moments, the bridge of trust is fortified, strong enough to bear the weight of our shared experiences.

But trust, much like any other prized possession, is fragile. Imagine a glass vase, elegant and pristine. Deceit or betrayal can shatter this vase, much like it can erode the trust built over the years. And while one might piece together the broken shards, the vase never regains its original form. Once trust is broken, the scars remain as a reminder of past wounds.

Maintaining trust takes some work. What can be done to make sure it remains intact?

Communication is the golden key. The thread stitches together the fabric of trust when it threatens to tear apart. Open dialogue, heart-to-heart conversations, and a willingness to listen are essential. It's crucial to voice concerns, share feelings, and address any dissonance before it grows into an irreparable rift. The beauty of trust lies in its ability to be nurtured through honest conversations.

Equally important is the act of accountability. To err is human, but to own up to one's mistakes is divine. Whether it's a forgotten promise or a significant blunder, taking responsibility and making genuine amends is a testament to one's character. It sends a clear message: "I value our relationship more than my pride."

Consistency, too, is the lifeblood of trust

Occasional grand gestures might impress, but day-to-day acts of kindness, understanding, and reliability cement trust. It knows that come rain or shine; the other person will stand by your side, unwavering.

Invest time and effort in the relationship. Trust flourishes when nurtured with care, love, and understanding, like a plant that needs water and sunlight. Making time for the other person, cherishing shared moments, and creating memories fortifies the bond.

To sum it up, trust is not just an emotion; it's a commitment, a promise to be there on sunny days and stormy nights. Building and preserving it requires patience, dedication, and courage. It's the bridge that spans the gaps of our differences, the anchor that keeps our ships steady. In the ever-evolving dance of human connections, may trust be the rhythm that guides your steps, leading you to the symphony of genuine, enduring relationships.

Communication is Key

Once upon a time, humans found themselves in a perplexing dilemma in a world unlike the one we currently occupy. Without signs of communication, they were detached in a deep sea of uncertainty and misinterpretation. That is, until the art of communication was discovered, and it was as if the sun had risen for the first time, illuminating a world previously shrouded in darkness.

The power of communication lies in its simplicity. At its core, it's translating our internal universe into a language another person can understand. The bridge connects two minds and souls, allowing us to share, secure, and belong.

Imagine you're standing at the edge of a vast canyon. On the other side stands someone you care about. Between you lies a chasm of silence, misunderstandings, and unspoken emotions. Communication is the bridge that spans this divide. With every word, every gesture, and every shared moment, you lay down planks, getting closer to the other side. The beauty of this bridge is that it's not constructed of bricks and mortar but of understanding, empathy, and shared experiences.

But why is communication so vital, and what happens in its absence?

In the absence of effective communication, assumptions take root. Like wild weeds, they grow and multiply, clouding our judgments and perceptions. "She didn't call; she must be angry," or "He didn't appreciate my efforts; he doesn't care." These narratives spun from the threads of silence, are often far from the truth, leading to unnecessary heartache and distance.

Open communication clears the air, like a gentle wind sweeping away the clouds to reveal a clear blue sky. We offer the other person a glimpse into our world by expressing our thoughts, emotions, and concerns. It's like opening the windows of a house, letting in the fresh air and the sunshine, allowing for clarity and understanding.

Communication is the lifeline of personal growth and self-aware-ness. When we articulate our feelings, we're not just sharing them with someone else, but also clarifying them for ourselves. Putting emotions into words and defining our thoughts brings clarity, helping us navigate the maze of our psyche with more confidence.

And it's not just about the words we say; it's also about how we tell them. The tone, the body language, and the choice of words all play a pivotal role. Sometimes, a gentle touch, a reassuring smile, or a comforting hug communicate more than a thousand words ever could.

Proper communication is as much about listening as speaking. In the busyness of today's world, where everyone is eager to be heard, the art of listening is slowly becoming a lost treasure. To truly listen is to give someone the gift of your undivided attention, to be a silent witness to their joys, sorrows, hopes, and fears. The seeds of deep connections are sown in these quiet moments of listening.

In relationships, be they personal or professional, influential com-munication acts as a bomb, soothing frayed nerves, resolving conflicts, and fostering an environment of mutual respect. The compass guides us through the stormy seas of disagreements, leading us to the shores of understanding.

Yet, in today's digital age, with screens often becoming our primary mode of communication, we find ourselves at a curious crossroads. On the one hand, technology has bridged distances, allowing us to con-nect with someone thousands of miles away at the click of a button. On the other hand, it poses the risk of creating emotional distances, with emojis replacing genuine emotions and texts, sometimes lacking the warmth of a human voice.

So, how can we ensure that we effectively harness the power of communication in this digital era?

Firstly, be present. Whether you're chatting over a coffee or a phone, give the other person your full attention. Let them know they matter at that moment and that their words and emotions hold value.

Secondly, cultivate the art of active listening. Instead of formulating your response while the other person is still speaking, truly listen to what they're saying. Dive beneath the surface of their words, seeking the emotions and intentions that lie beneath.

Lastly, practice empathy. Before responding, especially in moments of conflict, take a moment to step into the other person's shoes. Seeing the world from their perspective can pave the way for more compassionate and effective communication.

Communication is the key that unlocks the doors of understanding, empathy, and connection. The melody adds rhythm to the dance of human interactions, ensuring that even in silence, our hearts resonate with shared emotions. In the grand scheme of life, let communication be the glue that holds relationships together.

Chapter 9

In the heart of Paris, an obscure art gallery is tucked away from the usual tourist trails. It showcases what most would consider an unusual exhibition–a collection of "failed" pieces by renowned artists. Works of art that, at first glance, seem flawed, unfinished, or downright mistakes. But look closer, and you'll see the raw, untamed genius in each stroke, each misshapen form.

Why would anyone create a space to celebrate perceived "failures"?

Because, in reality, these so-called missteps in art parallel the journey of life. Just as each flawed artwork has a backstory of effort, vision, and evolution, our failures, too, have profound stories to tell. They are the milestones, albeit uncomfortable, on our road to success.

When Thomas Edison tried inventing the light bulb, he encountered multiple setbacks. Famously, he once remarked, "I didn't mess up. I recently discovered 10,000 methods that won't work." Edison knew that behind every failure was a lesson and, behind every class, a stepping stone toward success.

Let's explore the concept of failure and understand how reframing it can unlock doors we never knew existed.

Imagine young Emma, a talented pianist. She practices diligently for an upcoming concert. The day arrives, her fingers poised on the keys, the audience in expectant silence. But halfway through, she fumbles, losing her rhythm and flow. Embarrassed, she finishes her piece amidst muted applause.

Most would view this as a failure. But let's reframe.

Devastated, Emma could focus on her mistake and let it deter her from ever performing again. Or she could reflect, identify what went wrong, and strategize how to avoid it in the future. The latter approach transforms a faltering performance into a profound learning experience. That's the power of reframing failure.

Our society often paints success in broad strokes of accomplishments and accolades. Failure, conversely, is hushed, hidden away, a source of shame. But what if we viewed failure not as the opposite of success but as a part of it?

The famed Harry Potter author JK Rowling was no stranger to failure. Publishers rejected her stories multiple times before her iconic novels saw the light of day. Rowling, however, chose to persevere, to take those rejections as signs that she needed to push harder and refine more. In reframing her failures, she paved her way to unprecedented literary success.

When we experience failure, it's essential to remember three things:

Everyone Fails: No matter how polished someone's life may seem; everyone has faced adversity at some point. It's a universal experience, and you're not alone.

Failures are Lessons: Like Edison's experiments or Rowling's manuscript rejections, failures teach us what doesn't work, guiding us towards what might. They hone our skills, sharpen our instincts, and make us resilient.

It's Temporary: Failure is not a permanent state. It's a moment, an event, a chapter, not the entire story. How you choose to proceed after a setback determines the plot ahead.

History is filled with figures who reframed failure, turning it into a launchpad for success. Abraham Lincoln faced many electoral defeats before becoming one of the most celebrated presidents of the United States. Before becoming a media mogul, Oprah Winfrey was deemed "unfit for TV."

It's vital to shift our perspective. Instead of dreading failure, anticipate it as an inevitable, even welcome, guest on your journey. When it arrives, greet it, learn from it, and then bid it farewell as you would with any transient visitor.

Consider going back to that Parisian gallery. Among the "failed" artworks, there's a piece by an artist who tried to capture the sunset but felt he couldn't get the hues right. Yet, the resulting blend of colors, while not a conventional evening, exudes a unique, breathtaking beauty of its own.

Similarly, in our lives, when plans go awry and results don't align with our expectations, we often create unexpectedly beautiful outcomes. By reframing failure, we pave the way for future successes and craft stories and experiences that are uniquely, imperfectly, ours.

In life's big picture, threads of failure interweave with those of success, creating a masterpiece that is as rich in lessons as it is in achievements. So, the next time you stumble, remember: it's not the fall that defines you, but how you rise after it. And in that rising, in that reframing, lies the true essence of success.

Coping Mechanisms and Moving Forward

Life is an unpredictable journey composed of a mixture of joyous highs, sorrowful lows, achievements, and hardships. These moments blend together to form the unique fabric of our lives. There's no single roadmap or user manual, and often, we find ourselves navigating through the maze of emotions, uncertainties, and challenges using our intuition and the tools we've gathered over time.

Amelia, a passionate traveler, often found solace in the lap of mountains. She loved the predictability of urban life, but the hills, with their unexpected storms and serene valleys, mirrored life itself. During one of her expeditions, she encountered a sudden, furious storm. With no shelter in sight, Amelia was left with two choices: panic or adapt. Drawing upon her experiences, she built a makeshift shelter and waited out the storm. When dawn broke, the mountains stood majestic and unwavering, bearing no trace of the previous night's turmoil. Amelia emerged stronger, wiser, and even more in awe of nature's resilience.

Life's adversities are much like Amelia's unexpected storm. They appear without warning, testing our limits and often leaving us feeling lost and overwhelmed. However, within us lie the tools and coping mechanisms to weather these storms and move forward.

In moments of crisis, our minds can become our sanctuaries, provided we've nurtured them well. Coping mechanisms are mental, emotional, and sometimes physical strategies that help us navigate stress, trauma, and everyday challenges. While the journey is deeply personal, the lessons we gather are universal.

Imagine a river flowing with a steady current for a moment, suddenly meeting a colossal boulder. The water doesn't stop. It finds its way over, around, or beneath the obstruction, constantly moving forward. Our psyche operates similarly. When faced with obstacles, it instinctively searches for pathways to cope and progress.

Let's delve deeper into understanding these pathways.

The most profound emotions often emerge from experiences of loss, trauma, or significant life changes. The grief of losing a loved one, the aftermath of a broken relationship, and the anxiety of a career shift are but a few of life's profound challenges. In these moments, our inner dialogue plays a pivotal role. By recognizing and acknowledging our emotions, we permit ourselves to heal. Suppressed feelings, on the other hand, often resurface, intensifying our distress.

Human connections are another powerful coping mechanism. In a world increasingly driven by virtual interactions, genuine, heart-to-heart conversations have become rare yet are profoundly healing. Sharing our vulnerabilities, fears, and hopes creates a bond of mutual understanding and support. Remember that asking for help is not a show of weakness, but a testament to our strength and self-awareness.

The natural world can be a source of comfort. The ocean's rhythmical shift from high tide to low, the gentle noise of leaves in a tranquil wood, and simply gazing up at the endless starry sky offers a viewpoint that helps ease our worries. Nature reminds us of the transience of life's problems and the eternal cycle of creation and recreation.

Then some activities immerse us, taking our minds off distressing thoughts and channeling our energies into creation and productivity. Art, music, writing, and many other hobbies can be therapeutic. These acts of creation, however small, provide a sense of accomplishment and purpose.

Life, however, is not about merely coping. It's about thriving. The journey forward remains once the storm has passed and the immediate pain has dulled. Moving forward isn't about forgetting or negating our past experiences. It's about integrating them into our narrative, drawing strength from them, and building a future anchored in hope and resilience.

Amelia's experience on that stormy mountain night didn't deter her from her subsequent expeditions. Instead, it enriched her travels, prepared her more, and deepened her bond with the mountains. Similarly, our adversities and the coping mechanisms we employ add depth to our character, making us more empathetic, robust, and wise.

As we navigate the winding roads of life, it's essential to remember that our coping mechanisms are our companions, guiding us, supporting us, and ensuring that no matter how fierce the storm, we emerge from it with grace, wisdom, and an unyielding spirit.

In the end, life's journey is as much about the challenges we face as it is about how we overcome them. As we move forward, with each step and coping strategy, we write a story of courage, resilience, and indomitable spirit. A story uniquely ours, yet universally relatable, echoing the timeless dance of struggle and triumph.

Drawing Strength from Past Experiences

In the dimly lit room of an old countryside home, Eleanor sat, immersed in a diary she hadn't opened in years. As the fading evening sun filtered through the weathered curtains, the pages whispered stories from her past - moments of euphoria, heartbreak, adventures, and ordinary days that seemed extraordinarily significant in retrospect. Each entry was more than just a memory; it was a piece of a puzzle that had shaped her into the woman she had become.

The past is a powerful entity, a vast expanse that stretches behind each of us, littered with milestones, choices, and lessons. While some memories make us smile, others may carry the weight of regret, sadness, or pain. However, every experience, good or bad, offers insights and learnings. Drawing strength from these past experiences is like extracting gold from ore; it's about recognizing the value within the rubble.

For Eleanor, revisiting her diary was a journey of self-realization. Everything held a lesson in her childhood dreams, the mistakes she made, the paths she chose, and those she abandoned. Here, amidst the inked words, she discovered that her past was not just a timeline but a treasure trove of wisdom and strength.

We all carry our histories, though only sometimes inked on paper. And while the past can't be changed, it can be revisited with a perspective that seeks growth and understanding. Every experience offers an opportunity to learn; even our darkest moments can illuminate our path forward, provided we choose to see them in that light.

Consider heartbreak, for instance. Almost everyone, at some point, has felt the sting of a relationship that didn't work out. While the immediate aftermath is pain, upon reflection, heartbreak often teaches resilience, self-worth, and the importance of moving on. Similarly, failures, whether in personal ambitions or professional pursuits, may initially wound our pride. But when viewed through the lens of growth, these failures become lessons in perseverance, adaptability, and humility.

Strength isn't always derived from triumphant moments. Often, it's the adversities that carve out our core, molding us into resilient beings. It's during the turbulent phases that we discover our boundaries, our passions, and our capabilities. It's like steel forged in fire; the high temperatures don't weaken it but make it more challenging, sharper, and refined.

However, it's crucial to remember that drawing strength from past experiences is about something other than dwelling on what was. It's about understanding and leveraging those experiences to enhance the present and future. Like a sailor using the stars to navigate, our past can guide us, but it shouldn't dictate our journey.

There are a few gentle ways to embark on this process:

Reflection, not Regret: Look back at your experiences not with regret but with a spirit of thought. Understand your choices, appreciate the lessons, and release burdensome guilt or resentment.

Share and Listen: Often, sharing your stories and listening to others helps put things in perspective. It's therapeutic and builds a sense of camaraderie. Every individual is a repository of experiences, and there's immense wisdom in collective histories.

Acknowledge Growth: Recognize the person you've become because of your experiences. Celebrate the growth, the scars, the wisdom, and the stories that have shaped you.

Use it as Fuel: Every experience, especially the challenging ones, adds to your reservoir of strength. Draw from this reservoir when faced with new challenges. Remind yourself of past triumphs over adversity.

For Eleanor, as she closed her diary, the sun had set, enveloping the room in gentle darkness. But within her was a light, kindled by her past and shining brightly toward her future. With a smile, she realized that her past wasn't something to escape from, but a foundation she could build, drawing strength, wisdom, and courage.

Similarly, as we tread the path of life, it's essential to understand that our past is an ally. Every joy, every tear, every stumble, and every victory has contributed to the fabric of our being. It's a testament to our journey, filled with complexities, colors, patterns, and, most importantly, stories that define us. And as we move forward, these stories and experiences will be our compass, guide, and strength.

Chapter 10

I n almost all individual success stories, one figure stands out as an essential guidepost—the mentor. For some, this might evoke an image of an older, wiser individual imparting wisdom to a younger protégé. For others, a mentor might be a peer, offering a fresh perspective or valuable expertise. Mentors come in all shapes and sizes, and their influence is indispensable.

Think back to the first time you rode a bike. Perhaps there was an adult—maybe a parent—holding the back of your seat, helping you balance as you pedaled. They provided the necessary guidance and support until you could venture forth independently. Similarly, as we travel the pathways of our personal and professional lives, mentors act as our stabilizers, ensuring that while we might wobble, we won't fall.

One might ask why it's so critical to have a mentor.

First and foremost, mentors have "been there, done that." They've traveled similar roads, stumbled over the same obstacles, and celebrated comparable successes. This experience equips them with a depth of insight that's both rare and valuable. They can anticipate potential pitfalls and guide navigating complex situations. When faced with a crossroads, the wisdom of someone who has journeyed before us can be the light that helps us choose the right path.

Mentors offer a fresh perspective—a bird's eye view, if you will. When deeply entrenched in a situation, our vision can become short-sighted. We might become overwhelmed, unable to distinguish the forest from the trees. A mentor, however, can provide clarity. They can identify patterns we might miss, connect dots innovatively, and offer solutions that might not have occurred to us. It's not about them having all the answers, but rather about them asking the right questions.

In addition to knowledge and perspective, mentors provide a sense of accountability. There's an unspoken commitment when you share your goals or aspirations with a mentor. They become stakeholders in your journey, and their belief in your potential can drive you to strive harder and achieve more. Being aware that someone cares about your success, cheering from the sidelines, can be the motivational boost that propels you forward, especially during challenging times.

But the mentor-mentee relationship isn't just about guidance; it's about empowerment. Excellent mentors don't just offer solutions; they teach you how to find them. They challenge your assumptions, prompt you to think critically, and encourage you to trust your instincts. Over time, this builds not only your problem-solving skills but also your confidence. You learn to stand on your own two feet, making informed decisions rooted in your mentor's wisdom and personal experience.

Let's also talk about networks in today's interconnected world; who you know can be as crucial as what you know. With their years of experience, mentors usually have extensive networks spanning various industries and domains. They can make introductions, open doors to opportunities, and offer endorsements that can significantly accelerate your growth trajectory.

One of the most underrated aspects of mentorship is the emotional support mentors provide. The road to personal and professional fulfillment is riddled with highs and lows. There are moments of exhilarating success and periods of disheartening setbacks. In these roller-coaster experiences, a mentor can be a pillar of support. They celebrate your achievements, offering praise and validation. And during tough times, they encourage you, reminding you of your potential and reassuring you that setbacks are just stepping stones to success.

However, for all its benefits, mentorship is not a one-size-fits-all solution. The mentor-mentee relationship is deeply personal and rooted in mutual respect and trust. It requires effort from both sides—open communication, active listening, and a commitment to growth. It's a symbiotic relationship, with both parties learning and evolving together.

While life's journey is unique to every individual, the challenges, dilemmas, and choices we encounter are often universal. In navigating this journey, a mentor can be the compass that offers direction and clarity. They provide knowledge, instill confidence, open doors, and offer unwavering support. So, as we chart our paths, seeking a mentor isn't just a choice—it's a necessity.

Finding and Connecting with the Right Mentor

Mentorship is an age-old tradition, a beautiful dance between experience and enthusiasm, wisdom and wonder. Across history's pages, we find tales of mentors and their protégés: Socrates and Plato, Dumbledore and Harry, Mr. Miyagi, and Daniel. These relationships underscore the profound impact mentors can have on our growth, personally and professionally shaping us. Yet, one key question often lingers: How does one find and connect with the right mentor?

Embarking on the journey of seeking a mentor can feel daunting. However, with the right approach and mindset, navigating these waters and discovering a guiding star that resonates with your unique aspirations and goals is possible.

Know Yourself First

Before embarking on the quest for a mentor, engage in some introspection. Understand your motivations, aspirations, strengths, and areas of growth. What are you hoping to gain from this mentorship? Is it skill development, industry insights, career guidance, or simply a sounding board? Your clarity becomes the beacon that attracts the right mentor.

Cast a Wide Net but Fish with Precision

While it's tempting to zero in on a high-profile industry leader or someone with an impressive title, remember that the most influential mentors are those whose values, experiences, and expertise align with your journey. Start by identifying potential mentors within your immediate network—colleagues, professors, family friends. Then, expand your horizon to industry events, workshops, and online platforms. Mentors can also take the shape of an author or expert whose style and story resonate.

While casting a wide net can introduce you to a diverse pool of potential mentors, it's essential to fish with precision. Tailor your approach to each individual, demonstrating a genuine interest in their experiences and insights. Ask yourself these questions. Have they done what I want to do? Do they know what I want to learn?

Make the First Move

The act of reaching out can feel intimidating. However, remember that most accomplished individuals understand the value of mentorship because they've been mentored. Draft a concise, genuine message explaining who you are, what you admire about them, and why you believe their guidance would be invaluable. This isn't a sales pitch; it's an invitation to a mutually enriching relationship. And while not everyone might respond or be available, don't get disheartened. The right connections often manifest when we least expect them.

Seek a Relationship, Not Just Guidance

Mentorship is not a transaction; it's a relationship. While mentors can offer a wealth of knowledge and insights, it's crucial to cultivate a bond founded on mutual respect, trust, and understanding. Share your experiences, challenges, and successes. Engage in open dialogue, ask questions, and actively listen. Over time, as trust deepens, you'll find that the relationship evolves, offering not just guidance but emotional support, encouragement, and empowerment.

Offer Value in Return

Mentorship isn't a one-way street. While mentors offer their time, expertise, and advice, mentees can provide fresh perspectives, enthusiasm, and expertise in areas the mentor might need to become more familiar with. Whether sharing insights from a recent course, offering a unique viewpoint, or assisting with a project, seek ways to enrich the relationship, making it mutually beneficial.

Embrace Vulnerability

Authentic mentor-mentee relationships thrive on openness. Be willing to share your fears, uncertainties, and failures. Vulnerability fosters deep connection and understanding. It also allows mentors to offer tailored guidance, helping you navigate challenges with resilience and grace.

Commit to Growth

Finding the right mentor is just the beginning. The true essence of mentorship lies in growth. Act on the advice you receive, seek feedback, and consistently challenge yourself. Demonstrating commitment, initiative, and a hunger for change enriches your journey and reinforces the mentor's belief in your potential.

Celebrate and Reflect

As milestones are achieved, and challenges are overcome, take a moment to celebrate and reflect. Share your successes with your mentor, acknowledging their role in your journey. Such moments of celebration deepen the bond, fostering gratitude and mutual admiration.

Finding and connecting with the right mentor is a transformative experience. It's a journey of discovery, growth, and profound connection. While the path may have its share of twists and turns, the destination—a meaningful mentor-mentee relationship—makes every step worthwhile. As you stand at the shoreline of mentorship, remember that the ocean's depths hold treasures beyond imagination. Dive in with purpose, authenticity, and an open heart, and watch as the waves lead you to your guiding star.

Being a Mentor to Others

While many of us have been fortunate to receive guidance from others, there comes a time when the roles reverse, and we are presented with the opportunity to light the path for someone else. Being a mentor is not merely a title, but a responsibility and a privilege.

Often, the image of a mentor is one of age and wisdom, etched with lines of experience. However, age is not the only qualifier. At its core, mentorship is about possessing a willingness to share, a listening capacity, and a heart that genuinely cares.

Imagine, for a moment, a young tree—a sapling, fragile and new. Alone, it faces challenges from the elements, but under the shelter of an older tree, it finds shade, protection, and the chance to grow stronger. Such is the nature of mentorship. It's about providing shelter, nourishment, and knowledge, allowing the mentee to flourish.

But what does it mean to be a mentor, and how can one truly embrace this role? Let's delve into the intricacies of this journey.

The Heart of Listening

One of the most crucial aspects of mentorship is the ability to listen actively. A listening ear is a rare sanctuary in a world bursting with noise. Mentees, especially those just starting their journey, often grapple with doubts, fears, and dreams that swirl in their minds. As a mentor, offering them a space where they are heard, understood, and not judged becomes the foundation of trust.

Sharing the Light and Shadows

While it's tempting to share only the successes, proper mentorship involves shedding light on failures as well. The most potent lessons lie in the shadows of our past mistakes. By discussing the times we stumbled, the decisions we regret, and the lessons we learned, we arm our mentees with the foresight to navigate similar challenges.

Guidance, Not Dictation

A mentor's role is not to dictate the path but to guide. It's essential to balance offering advice and allowing the mentee to make decisions. Please share your insights and give them the tools and knowledge but remember to let them carve out their journey. This approach ensures they grow confidently, make decisions, and learn from their successes and mistakes.

The Mirror Effect

One of the most profound gifts a mentor can offer is reflection. Sometimes, a mentee needs someone to mirror their thoughts, feelings, and aspirations, helping them see things more clearly. By reflecting on their ideas with added insights and perspectives, you can help them refine their vision and goals.

Evolving Together

Mentorship is not a static relationship. As time progresses, the dynamics may shift. There will be moments when the mentee brings new knowledge, challenges your perspectives, or teaches you something new. Embrace these moments. They signify the beauty of mutual growth.

Empathy

At the heart of every mentor-mentee relationship lies a thread of empathy. It's the ability to put oneself in another's shoes and feel their excitement, fears, and aspirations. Selflessness ensures that your guidance is tailored to the mentee's unique journey, ensuring it resonates deeply with them.

Releasing the mentee

One of the most challenging parts of mentorship is recognizing when to let go. There comes a time in every mentee's journey when they are prepared to soar and extend their wings. As mentors, while the instinct might be to protect and guide indefinitely, true success lies in acknowledging this moment and releasing them to embrace their destiny.

Being a mentor is a journey of profound significance. It's about nurturing, guiding, and eventually letting go. But, above all, it's about legacy. Long after our chapters end, the echoes of our guidance, the wisdom we shared, and the seeds of belief we planted continue to thrive in those we mentored. In mentoring, we discover the eternal truth—through giving, we receive; through guiding, we learn; and through sharing, our lives find more profound meaning and purpose.

Chapter 11

V era stood on the beach, the surf tickling her toes and creating intricate designs in the sand that disappeared just as quickly as they had formed. It wasn't just the serenity of the beach that had brought her here, but the memories of her grandfather. He'd often spoken of how the ocean made him reflect on the legacy he would leave behind. Today, Vera was on the same quest, wondering about the imprints she would go in the sands of time.

When discussing legacy, our minds often drift to grand gestures, vast fortunes, or famous contributions to humankind. However, the beauty of heritage lies in its subjective nature. It's personal. It's about each individual's unique mark on the world.

The Whisper of Generations Past

Legacy, in its essence, isn't something tangible. The echo of our actions, beliefs, and values reverberates through time. It's the lessons Vera's grandfather taught her, the stories he shared, and the values he lived by. These intangibles, woven into the fabric of her being, became the compass guiding her life.

Understanding the Weight of Choices

Every choice we make, whether grand or small, adds a brushstroke to the canvas of our legacy. Think of Rosa Parks. Her decision not to give up her seat wasn't a pre-planned grand gesture for posterity. It was a simple, momentary choice that reflected her values and beliefs. Yet, it was a choice that changed the course of history.

Similarly, when Vera chose to volunteer at the local community center or when she decided to adopt a sustainable lifestyle, she wasn't thinking about legacy. She was merely living her truth. However, these choices, bit by bit, were crafting her legacy.

Redefining Legacy in the Digital Age

In this era of digital footprints, our legacy takes on another dimension. Every tweet, every photo, and every blog post add to the digital representation of our lives. Vera realized that her online persona was also a reflection of her legacy. It wasn't about curating a perfect image, but ensuring that her digital self authentically represented her values and beliefs.

The Ripple Effect: Legacy is about Influence

Legacy isn't confined to our direct actions. It's about the ripples we create. Vera remembered her grandfather's tales, not of his achievements but of the lives he touched. The tree he planted became the community's favorite gathering spot, the scholarship he funded that helped a young girl become the first doctor in her village, and the letters he wrote that inspired his family across generations.

In her journey, Vera realized that her legacy would be the lives she touched, the inspiration she sparked, and the changes she catalyzed, directly or indirectly.

Crafting a Legacy: It's an Ongoing Journey

One doesn't wake up one day and decide, "Today, I will create my legacy." Legacy is crafted every day through every interaction, every decision, every dream, and every challenge faced. It's about the kind of person we choose to be and the values we choose to uphold.

Vera's musings by the ocean that day were profound, not because she found definitive answers, but because she began the journey of introspection. By questioning, reflecting, and understanding her desires for the legacy she wished to leave behind, she took the first step toward creating it.

Embracing the Fluidity of Legacy

Legacy is not static. It evolves as we evolve. The beauty of this journey is that we can always choose to change, adapt, and grow. Our past adds to our legacy, but our future holds the potential to shape it in ways we might not yet even comprehend.

Conclusion: Your Legacy, Your Masterpiece

Vera felt a quiet determination as the sun dipped below the horizon, casting a golden hue over everything. She realized that legacy wasn't about the end but the journey. It was about living a life so rich in experiences, values, and connections that it left an indelible mark on the world.

Your legacy, like Vera's, is your masterpiece. It's a reflection of your life's journey, your beliefs, your dreams, and your aspirations. It's intimate, personal, and profound. As you navigate the voyage of life, ask yourself: What legacy am I creating? And remember, it's never too late to craft the legacy you dream of. Each day offers a new beginning, a fresh canvas waiting for your brushstrokes.

Setting Long-Term Personal and Professional Goals

Among the monotony of daily routines, the call of immediate deadlines, and the allure of short-term rewards, it's easy to lose sight of the bigger picture. Like a sailor without a compass, we can find ourselves adrift in the vast ocean of life, tossed by waves of circumstances, often reactive rather than proactive. This is where the magic of setting long-term personal and professional goals comes into play.

The Weaving of Dreams

Imagine for a moment that life is a handmade blanket. Each thread represents a dream, an aspiration, or a goal. Some lines are short-lived, expressing fleeting desires. But the ones who traverse this tapestry's length, adding depth and structure, are our long-term goals. They guide our life's design, clarifying our purpose and passion.

Jasmine, a young professional in the corporate world, was lost in her daily responsibilities. While excelling at her tasks and climbing the corporate ladder, a nagging feeling persisted that she was missing something. This feeling was the absence of those long threads in her life's tapestry. She had yet to set long-term goals.

Unearthing Desires: The Personal Quest

Setting personal long-term goals starts with introspection. It's about peeling back the layers of external expectations and societal norms to unearth what truly matters to us.

For Jasmine, this meant taking a sabbatical. She backpacked through Europe, seeking the beauty of different cultures and the essence of her desires. What did she want from life in the next decade? Was it a family? Mastery in a hobby? Financial independence? By the time she returned, Jasmine had answers. She realized she wanted to write a book, learn the art of pottery, and build a home by age 40.

Professional Ambitions: Beyond Job Titles

Professional goals are often misconstrued as merely climbing up job titles. While career progression is essential, long-term professional goals dive deeper. They encompass the skills we wish to acquire, the impact we want to make in our field, and the balance we seek between our professional and personal lives.

With her newfound clarity, Jasmine returned to her job with a vision. She wanted to lead projects that had a social impact. She sought mentorship to master skills that weren't just about her current role, but about where she envisioned herself a decade later. Jasmine didn't just aspire to be a 'Director' or 'VP'; she aspired to be a change-maker.

The Roadmap to Dreams

Setting goals is just the beginning. The real challenge lies in crafting a roadmap to achieve them. This is where strategy meets passion. It's about breaking down these long-term goals into medium and short-term milestones. It's about being realistic about challenges and yet optimistic about possibilities.

Jasmine's goal of writing a book seemed daunting initially. But she broke it down: Year one was about attending workshops, year two for outlining and drafting, year three for revisions, and so on. Similarly, her professional goals were dissected into actionable steps over months and years.

The Dynamic Nature of Goals

It's essential to understand that goals aren't set in stone. They are dynamic, evolving as we grow and as our circumstances change. What's crucial is to regularly revisit them, ensuring they still resonate with our desires and adjusting them as needed.

Two years into her journey, Jasmine realized pottery wasn't her passion. Instead, she was drawn toward customer service. She allowed herself the flexibility to change that personal goal, understanding that the essence was in finding joy and not sticking to a predetermined path.

Commitment, Patience, and Resilience

The journey towards long-term goals is rarely a straight one. It's filled with obstacles, moments of self-doubt, and external pressures. The keys to navigating this journey are commitment, patience, and resilience. It's about staying committed to the vision, having the patience to allow dreams to manifest in their own time, and the strength to bounce back from setbacks.

Jasmine faced numerous rejections from publishers for her book. But she persisted, refining her work, seeking feedback, and, most importantly, believing in her story. Four years later, not only was her book published, but it also became a bestseller.

The Horizon of Possibilities

Setting long-term personal and professional goals isn't a task to check off a list. It's a continuous journey of self-discovery, growth, and evolution. It's about gazing at the horizon of possibilities, choosing a direction, setting sail, and adjusting the course.

Jasmine's life transformed not because she achieved all her goals, but because she had them. They gave her purpose, direction, and a zest for life. They made her proactive, turning her from a passive participant in life's journey to an active architect of her destiny.

Keeping your dreams fresh in your mind will give them depth, beauty, and purpose.

Creating a Lasting Impact

What does leaving a lasting impact on a world saturated with fleeting moments, viral trends, and brief stories mean? How do we carve our niche, etching our presence in ways that outlive our transient existence? Let's embark on this introspective journey, exploring the art and essence of creating a difference that truly stands the test of time.

The Measure of Impact

Historical figures like Nelson Mandela, Mother Teresa, or Leonardo da Vinci might come to mind when we think of lasting impact. Their contributions shaped civilizations, crafted paradigms, and kindled revolutions. Yet, the effect is more than just the realm of world leaders or prodigious talents. Impact becomes synonymous with everyday heroes, like the teachers who shape mindsets, and mothers who instill values into their children's lives. Creating a lasting impact isn't about scale; it's about depth. It's not just about touching many lives but touching lives profoundly.

The Seeds of Purpose

Every impactful journey begins with self-awareness. Before influencing the world, we must discern our center of gravity—our purpose. It's the compass that guides our actions, ensuring they are rooted in authenticity and passion.

Consider Alana, a journalist by profession. She wasn't just content with reporting news; she yearned to share stories, bridging divides and fostering understanding. By understanding her purpose, she undertook projects that highlighted underrepresented voices, leaving a lasting impact on her readers and subjects alike.

The Symphony of Actions and Intentions

The impact is the symphony of our actions and intentions. It's not just about what we do, but also why and how we do it. Authentic choices amplify our efforts, granting them a weight that reverberates through time. It's why some seemingly small gestures are remembered and cherished long after grandiose deeds are forgotten.

Reflect on the story of an older man planting saplings in a deforested area. When questioned why he toiled so hard for trees that might not benefit him, he replied, "I live today because of trees planted by someone before me. I plant these for the future." His act was simple, but the intention was profound, ensuring his impact would echo across generations.

The Currency of Connections

Humans are intrinsically social beings entwined in a web of relationships. Thus, the lasting impact often flows through the channels of these connections. It's about what we offer the world and how we empower others to continue the legacy.

Returning to Alana's narrative, she realized that she needed to mentor the next generation of journalists to amplify her impact. By imparting skills, ethics, and passion, she wasn't just creating stories; she was shaping storytellers, ensuring her impact would ripple through their work.

The Grace of Giving

Leaving a lasting impact often converges on one elemental truth: the grace of giving. It's about transcending the self, reaching out with generosity, compassion, and love. Whether it's imparting knowledge, sharing resources, or simply offering a listening ear, the acts of giving, devoid of expectations, often bear the most enduring fruits.

Legacy Beyond Lifetimes

In our quest to create an impact, embracing life's impermanence is crucial. The beauty of influence lies in its ability to transcend our lifetimes. The trees we plant, the knowledge we share, the institutions we build, or the values we instill are the vessels that carry our legacy forward long after our footprints have faded from the sands of time.

So, what will your legacy be? How will you touch the world around you, leaving an indelible mark? Remember, every act, no matter how minor it seems, has the potential to create ripples. By anchoring ourselves purposefully, acting with authentic intentions, fostering connections, and embracing the grace of giving, we are leaving a legacy of which to be proud.

As you wander life's journey, reflect on this: It's not just about the years in our life, but the life in our years. By blending moments of meaning, purpose, and connection, we leave behind memories and a legacy, echoing the melody of our existence in the heartbeats of the world around us.

Chapter 12

L ife has an uncanny way of presenting itself as a series of chapters. When you think you've grasped the rhythm of a particular phase, a new one begins, often catching you off guard. These shifts, these passages of transformation, are referred to as life transitions.

Transitions aren't merely external changes in circumstances, like moving to a new city or starting a new job. They're deeply personal evolutions, altering not just our outer world but our inner landscape as well. They challenge our beliefs, perceptions, and identities, urging us to shed old skin and embrace the new.

As beautiful as the idea of growth and change sounds, grappling with life's transitions isn't always easy. A cocktail of excitement, anxiety, nostalgia, and hope often marks it. There's a bitter sweetness to leaving behind the known for the unknown, even if the former was less than perfect.

Picture yourself at the cliff's edge, the wind tousling your hair; the sun warming your skin, and an expansive, inviting ocean below. Jumping means diving into a new chapter, but it also means the comfort of the cliff's edge will be momentarily lost. This leap, this moment of suspension, embodies the essence of life's transitions.

So, how does one navigate these waters with grace and resilience?

The Grieving Process

Even positive transitions, like landing a dream job or entering a romantic relationship, come with their share of grief. There's a mourning for the past, the changing version of yourself, and the life that used to be. Recognizing and honoring this grief is crucial. Allow yourself to feel, reminisce, and process the emotions that bubble to the surface.

Embracing the Unknown

Uncertainty is a dominant theme in any transition. Instead of resisting it, one can embrace it as a doorway to possibilities. The unknown, though initially intimidating, is a blank canvas. It's an invitation to paint, to experiment, to explore. By adopting a curious mindset, the unease of not knowing can transform into an adventure of discovery.

Staying Anchored

In the throes of change, it's easy to feel disoriented. Here's where personal anchors become invaluable. These could be daily rituals, like morning meditation, weekly traditions, like a family dinner, or even cherished belongings that bring comfort. These anchors provide a sense of stability in the change, reminding you of your essence and grounding you on your journey.

Seeking Support

Transitioning can be isolating, especially when no one around you can relate to your experience. Remember that it's okay to seek support. Whether through friends, family, or professional counseling, sharing your feelings, fears, and hopes can provide clarity and relief. Often, just the act of articulating your thoughts can be cathartic.

Reframing the Narrative

How we perceive our transitions shapes our experience of them. If we view them as threats, they become sources of stress. But if we view them as opportunities for growth, they transform into adventures.

We can approach them with optimism and resilience by consciously choosing to reframe the narrative around life transitions.

Celebrating the Small Wins

Big transitions can be overwhelming, often making you feel lost. But even the most daunting transitions comprise smaller moments and milestones. Celebrating these small wins, be it adapting to a new environment, forging new relationships, or even just getting through a particularly challenging day, can inject positivity and motivation into the journey.

In the grand symphony of life, transitions are the crescendos, the moments of climax. They test us, reshape us, and, ultimately, enrich us. No matter how daunting, every transition is a bridge to a new version of ourselves. It's a reminder that life isn't static, and neither are we.

Understanding life transitions isn't just about navigating them; it's about savoring them, learning from them, and emerging from them with a deeper understanding of the self and the world. The adage goes, "What the caterpillar sees as the conclusion is just the beginning for the butterfly." So, here's to transitions, the endings they signify, and the beautiful beginnings they usher in.

Tools for Coping with Change

The universe has a rhythm, a heartbeat that pulses through galaxies, planets, and the core of human existence. At its essence, this rhythm is about change. Seasons change, civilizations rise and fall, and even the cells in our bodies regenerate, making us different people over decades.

While the difference is natural, it's not always easy to digest, especially when it catches us off guard.

Change can be exciting and intimidating, like moving to a new city, starting a new job, or ending a long-term relationship. But just as nature has its ways of transitioning through seasons, we too have tools and strategies to cope with life's ever-evolving change. The key lies not in resisting change but in flowing with it, understanding its nuances, and harnessing its transformative power.

At the heart of every change lies a lesson, a hidden message. If we resist change, we might miss this profound wisdom. Consider the metamorphosis of a butterfly: it doesn't resist its transformation but leans into it, and as a result, it emerges as one of nature's most beautiful creatures.

Wildly unexpected change can bring a whirlwind of emotions - fear, excitement, sadness, or even anger. It's essential to permit yourself to feel these emotions fully. Just as you wouldn't judge the weather for changing, don't judge yourself for having a natural human reaction to a shift in your environment or circumstances.

When faced with change, it's common to reminisce about "the good old days." Nostalgia has its charm, but it's also essential to remind oneself of the impermanence of life. For instance, the flowers that bloom in spring have their moment of glory and then make way for summer. Likewise, we must remember that life is a cycle of beginnings and endings; every end is a new beginning in disguise.

A helpful approach is to adopt a mindset of curiosity. Instead of seeing change as a disruption, view it as an exploration. When you're curious, you're open. And when you're available, you allow life's experiences to enrich, teach, and mold you. This doesn't mean the journey will always be comfortable, but it means it will be meaningful.

Practicing mindfulness can also be a beacon during times of change. By being present, by immersing yourself in the 'now,' you realize that life, at this moment, is okay. And if it's not, you also recognize that this moment will pass. This can be exceptionally comforting when the change you're experiencing feels overwhelming.

It's also crucial to maintain self-care routines. These act as anchors, providing stability during the process of changing. Whether it's a morning yoga routine, a nightly reading habit, or weekly catch-ups with friends, these rituals remind us of our essence and offer comfort during disruptive times.

Reach out and connect with others. Sharing your feelings and experiences can offer relief. Sometimes, merely putting your thoughts into words can provide clarity and perspective. Remember, while your experience is unique, the essence of change is universal, and there's solace in shared human experiences.

One of the most empowering tools is actively taking part in the change. Instead of being a passive recipient, take charge. For instance, if you're moving to a new city, try to explore it. Join community groups, participate in local activities, or take long walks to familiarize yourself with your new environment. By actively engaging, you transition from being at the mercy of change to being its co-creator.

Lastly, trust the journey. There's a broader narrative to life, a storyline that sometimes takes time to be visible. But if you look back, you'll often find that changes, even the most challenging ones, can lead you to places and experiences you'd never imagined. They carve out paths, introduce you to people, and present opportunities often aligned with your deepest desires and growth.

Change is as natural as the rise and fall of the sun. And just as nature has mechanisms to transition through its cycles, we, too, are equipped with innate wisdom and tools to navigate through life's ebb and flow.

By embracing change, flowing with it, and learning from it, we cope and thrive, making life much easier.

Celebrating Growth and Evolution

Life is full of highs and lows. We are on a unique journey, constantly evolving, growing, and transforming, just like the world around us.

Growth is a profound aspect of human existence. It's the heartbeat of life. Every dawn is a symbol of growth, a new beginning, and every sunset is a celebration of the day gone by. Yet, in the rush and routine of daily life, we often overlook this beautiful process of evolution that's taking place within us.

From the first words we spoke as toddlers to the complex decisions we make as adults, our life is a testament to continuous learning, adaptation, and evolution. But how often do we stop and honestly acknowledge this journey? How often do we take a moment to celebrate our growth?

Consider for a moment a tree. Year after year, it stands tall, facing the sun, the storms, and the changing seasons. And each year, it adds a new ring to its trunk, a mark of age, experiences, and growth. We, too, have proof of growth. Not visible, but rounds of experiences, wisdom, lessons learned, and challenges overcome.

Sometimes, our growth is evident in the significant milestones—graduating from college, getting that dream job, buying a house, or starting a family. But often, our most profound growth is subtle and silent. It's in the way we learn to manage our anger, in the way we become more empathetic, or in the manner we handle disappointments.

Yet, the irony of life is that we often remember failures more vividly than our successes. We obsess over what went wrong rather than what we learned from it. It's almost as if our minds are wired to focus on the negative, overshadowing the countless positive strides we've made.

But imagine if we could change this narrative. Imagine making it a habit to celebrate our growth, no matter how small or significant. What if, at the end of each day, we counted our blessings and growth moments instead of our troubles?

Celebrating growth is not about being arrogant or self-centered. It's about acknowledging the journey, and understanding that every experience, good or bad, has contributed to who we are today. It's about honoring the person we've become with all our imperfections and brilliance.

So, how do we celebrate this wondrous journey?

Begin with gratitude. Before the world wakes up each morning and the day's responsibilities kick in, take a few moments for yourself. Reflect on your journey, who you were, and who you're becoming. Thank the universe, or the higher power you believe in, for the strength, wisdom, and experiences that have shaped you.

Next, make it a point to share your growth stories. Narrate them to friends, write them in a journal, or perhaps share them on a blog. Stories have power—they inspire, they resonate, and they heal. And as you share your journey, you'll find that it uplifts others and reinforces your belief in your growth.

Invest in yourself with time and money. See every day as an opportunity to learn, to evolve. Attend workshops, listen to educational podcasts, read books, take courses, or engage in deep conversations. See the world with wonder, like a child, always curious, always eager to grow.

And while you're at it, celebrate others too. Recognize the growth in your friends, your family, and your colleagues. Compliment them, encourage them, and be their cheerleader. As we celebrate others, we uplift ourselves, too.

Lastly, be kind to yourself. Understand that growth is not linear. There will be days when you stumble, old patterns resurface, or challenges seem insurmountable. And that's okay. The growth journey is as much about the valleys as the peaks.

Life is a beautiful, meandering journey. It's an orchestra of experiences, emotions, learnings, and evolutions. And in this grand symphony, growth is the melody that binds it all. So, let's not just grow; let's celebrate every step, every leap, and every moment of this wondrous journey. Ultimately, it's not just about reaching a destination but about cherishing the journey and the person we become.

Chapter 13

In a bustling café on a rainy Saturday, Emily sat with her sketchbook. Around her, the world churned — the clink of coffee cups, the murmur of countless conversations, and the hum of life. But in her little world on paper, she was recreating the scene with strokes of charcoal. She wasn't a professional artist, nor did she aspire to be one. She was a software engineer who found solace in these stolen moments of creativity.

Our lives, often bound by routines, responsibilities, and the endless pursuit of practical goals, sometimes seem like colorful paintings. There's a predictability to our days that, while comforting, can feel stifling. Enter the world of creative outlets–those magical pursuits that lend color, texture, and vibrancy to our otherwise structured lives.

Emily's affair with sketching began as a child but took a backseat as academics, then a job took over. The monotony of coding, deadlines, and client meetings left her craving a release. Picking up the sketchbook one evening, she rediscovered the joy of translating thoughts onto paper. It became her sanctuary from stress.

Creative outlets aren't just hobbies but essential channels for expressing what words often cannot. Whether through painting, writing, dancing, singing, or even cooking, these activities allow us to process emotions, ideas, and experiences in a tangible form. They offer a refreshing break from our logical, analytical selves, letting the intuitive, imaginative parts of our brains take the lead.

Take Marcus, for instance, a banker by day. Numbers, data, and analysis were his world. But come evening, he would lose himself in the rhythm of the dance. As he swayed and spun in his salsa classes, the stresses of his day melted away. He wasn't doing it for any performance or accolade; it was a personal journey. The rhythm, the connection with a partner, and the joy of movement were therapeutic. Through dance, Marcus found a way to balance the rigidity of his profession with fluidity and freedom.

This balance is precisely why creative outlets are crucial. They act as counterweights to the demands of our daily lives. When bottled-up emotions, stress, or the monotony of routine threaten to overwhelm, these outlets become channels of release, ensuring mental and emotional well-being.

These pursuits can often lead to profound personal insights. By engaging in creative processes, we are, in many ways, conversing with our innermost selves. This dialogue can lead to heightened self-awareness, helping us better understand our aspirations, fears, and desires.

Jasmine, a school teacher, found this insight through writing. She penned her thoughts, experiences, and dreams every night in her journal. This ritual started as a simple diary entry, but over time; it evolved into a deeply reflective process. Through her words, she relived her experiences and began to see patterns, triggers, and growth areas in her life. Her journal became her mirror, reflecting her true self amidst the roles she played in her daily life.

Another compelling aspect of creative outlets is their ability to foster community. Shared passions bring people together, often forming bonds beyond the surface. Collaborative projects, group classes, or even online forums dedicated to specific crafts can lead to friendships and connections that enrich our lives.

In the heart of London, a group of individuals from diverse backgrounds comes together every weekend. Their binding factor? A shared love for pottery. As they mold and shape clay, they share stories, exchange ideas, and support one another. For many in this group, this isn't just about creating pottery; it's about finding a family away from home.

Creative outlets are not mere pastimes. They are lifelines that tether us to our authentic selves in a world that often demands conformity. They offer solace, joy, and a touch of magic, turning ordinary days into tapestries of memorable moments.

As Emily closed her sketchbook that day, she left the café with more than just a drawing. She carried a piece of her time, a moment where she was not defined by her job title, responsibilities, or societal expectations. She was simply Emily — the observer, the dreamer, the artist. In that fleeting moment, she had touched a part of her soul that no code could ever reach. And that, in its essence, is the magic of creative outlets.

Exploring Different Creative Mediums

Sophia had always been a storyteller, weaving tales for her little siblings during long summer nights. The power of words was her tool, and the infinite canvas of imagination was her playground. But one day, as she stumbled upon a quaint art studio in her town, she was introduced to an entirely new language of expression. There, she realized that creativity was not bound to one medium; it was an expansive universe waiting to be explored.

The world of creative mediums is like a vast, interconnected realm of pathways, each leading to a distinct garden of expression. Some of us, like Sophia, may have found comfort in one park, believing it to be our only haven. But venturing out and exploring different terrains can introduce us to new facets of ourselves we never knew existed.

Painting and Sketching: Walking into that art studio, Sophia felt the allure of colors. Painting is often considered the silent poetry of the soul. A brushstroke can communicate the depth of oceans and the vastness of skies. From the delicate watercolors that capture fleeting emotions to the boldness of acrylics that portray intense passion, painting is a dance between the mind, the hand, and the heart. It's not just about the end product but the process — the meditative rhythm of the brush on canvas, the blending of hues, and the freedom to make mistakes and start over.

Music: While at the studio, Sophia met Joshua, a musician. For him, music was the language of the cosmos. Every strum, beat, and note tells a story. Whether it's the sad tunes of a violin echoing with longing or the upbeat rhythm of drums celebrating life, music transcends barriers. It's a universal connector, bridging hearts across continents. And the beautiful part? One doesn't need to be a professional to experience its magic. Even humming a tune or tapping your foot can be cleansing.

Dance: Then there was Aria, who expressed through the fluidity of movement. Dance, for her, was freedom. It was about being in the moment, letting go of inhibitions, and allowing the body to speak its truth. Every dance form is a narrative, from ballet's graceful pirouettes to salsa's vibrant steps. And the stage? Well, it could be anywhere - a grand theater, a moonlit beach, or even the quiet confines of one's room.

Sculpture and Pottery: Beyond the conventional, there's the tactile world of sculpture and pottery. The act of molding clay or chiseling stone is powerfully grounding. It connects us to the essence of creation, where we play a tactile role in bringing form to thought. For artists like Leo, a sculptor Sophia met, it was about seeing the potential in raw material and patiently, lovingly shaping it into existence.

Digital Arts: Creativity has found new avenues in a world driven by technology. Digital art, animation, and graphic design have expanded the horizons of expression. These mediums allow for experimentation without boundaries. Imagine creating galaxies with a digital brush or designing worlds in the virtual realm. The fusion of tech and art is not just modern; it's revolutionary.

Literature and Writing: Sophia's first love, writing, had its unique charm. Words have the power to transport readers across time and space. From penning poems under starlit skies to crafting tales of adventures, writers are architects of dreams. It's a medium that demands vulnerability, for writing is to bare one's soul, hoping that someone resonates with your story somewhere.

Venturing into different mediums of creativity is not about mastering them all. It's about exploration, understanding, and growth. It's about realizing that creativity is not a box but a spectrum. And on this spectrum, there's room for everyone.

With her notebook filled with stories, Sophia now had a canvas splashed with colors. She realized that she was not just a storyteller through words, but also shades, tones, and textures. Her narratives found fresh voices.

To explore different creative mediums is to embrace the multifaceted nature of our being. It's about understanding that we, as humans, are innately versatile and capable of expressing ourselves in myriad ways. So, whether you find solace in the stroke of a brush, the rhythm of a song, the twirl of a dance, or the depth of words, remember, the world of creativity is vast, and its only limit is the sky of your imagination.

Turning Passion Projects into Income Streams

In the heart of a small town named Oakwood, there was an old bookstore called "Words and Dreams." For years, it was run by Mrs. Eleanor, an older woman with a twinkle in her eye and an insatiable love for books. Eleanor didn't just sell books; she wove tales around each one, making the buying experience magical.

Adjacent to the bookstore was a cozy café named "Cup & Quill," run by a young woman, Isabella. Isabella had a penchant for brewing the perfect cup of coffee and baking the most delectable pastries. But beyond that, she had a secret passion: crafting handmade journals.

Every evening after the cafe's shutter came down, Isabella would retreat to her little workshop at the back and immerse herself in crafting beautiful journals, each piece reflecting a part of her soul. They weren't just notebooks; they were stories waiting to be written.

One day, Eleanor wandered into the café after a particularly tiring day, hoping for a cup of coffee. She noticed a beautiful journal on the counter, its cover illustrated with intricate patterns. Eleanor was enchanted. "Is this for sale?" she inquired.

"Oh, that's just a little side project of mine," Isabella replied modestly.

Seeing an opportunity, Eleanor said, "How about we display some of your journals in my bookstore? I believe they would resonate with my customers."

Isabella hesitated. It was one thing to craft these journals as a passion but to monetize them; she was unsure. But Eleanor's belief in her talent and the lure of turning her love into a lucrative venture prompted her to agree.

The journals were an instant hit. Locals and visitors were enchanted by the books at "Words and Dreams" and the artisanal journals crafted by Isabella. Soon, the demand grew, and a small table display became a significant section of the store.

As weeks turned into months, Isabella realized she was onto something. With Eleanor's mentorship, she started refining her craft, introduced customization options, and even ventured into online sales.

One journal turned into ten, ten into a hundred, and before she knew it, "Cup & Quill" wasn't just a café; it was a brand synonymous with quality handmade journals.

Isabella's journey wasn't just about profit; it was about realizing the potential of a passion. Here's what we can glean from her experience:

Recognize the Value: Isabella initially viewed her journals as a hobby. It was Eleanor's external perspective that made her see their potential. Sometimes, we are too close to our passion projects to gauge their worth. Listening to feedback can open doors we never knew existed.

Start Small: Only some passion projects need a grand launch. Sometimes, starting small, as Isabella did by displaying a few journals in a local store, can be a stepping stone to more significant ventures.

Diversify: While the handmade touch was essential, Isabella realized customization was a lucrative avenue. Offering personalized products can tap into a niche market willing to pay a premium.

Seek Mentorship: Eleanor's business experience was instrumental in guiding Isabella. Having a mentor can provide insights, help avoid pitfalls, and capitalize on opportunities.

Evolve with Feedback: Isabella was open to feedback, tweaking her designs based on customer preferences. Being adaptable can keep the product relevant and in demand.

Stay True to the Essence: While business grew, Isabella ensured she never lost the soul of her journals. They remained artisanal, each crafted with love. Commercial pursuits should always uphold the essence of a passion project.

In time, Isabella's journals gained popularity far and wide. But more than the monetary gains, the joy of turning her dream into reality, her passion into a profession, was her real reward.

For many of us, our passions remain in the shadows, always a secondary pursuit. But as Isabella's story illustrates, passion projects can become thriving income streams with the right blend of belief, effort, and guidance. It's about seeing beyond the ordinary, recognizing potential, and taking that leap of faith.

And as for "Words and Dreams" and "Cup & Quill"? They stand side by side in Oakwood, a testament to dreams, dedication, and the magic that happens when the two intertwine.

Chapter 14

In a world driven by connections and collaborations, "networking" has become synonymous with success. Everywhere we turn, we hear the buzz of this term—be it in corporate hallways, educational seminars, or casual coffee meet-ups. They say networking is the key to opportunities, growth, and scaling the ladders of personal and professional accomplishment. But have you ever stopped to ask, what is networking, truly? Beyond the exchange of business cards and LinkedIn requests, what does it mean to actually network?

For many, networking provokes images of large conference halls, attendees adorned in crisp suits, holding wine glasses, and discussing their next big venture. Or perhaps it brings to mind those daunting corporate events where you're encouraged to mingle, share your elevator pitch, and showcase your professional prowess. And while these are certainly facets of networking, they are merely the proverbial tip of the iceberg.

At its core, networking is about human connection. It's about stories shared; experiences exchanged, and relationships built. It's not merely a transactional process, but a journey of understanding, learning, and growing together.

In an age where connections can be made with a simple click, the true essence of networking is often lost. We accumulate contacts, but how many of them do we genuinely know? How many have we spent hours with, discussing not just work but life, dreams, and aspirations? This is the foundation of true networking—the ability to see beyond professional titles and delve into the human behind them.

So, why do so many of us get it wrong? Perhaps because we've been conditioned to view networking as a means to an end. We're told it's a way to get that job, that client, or that promotion. And while these are potential outcomes, they should not be the driving force. Instead, networking should aim to forge genuine, long-lasting relationships.

Think back to the most memorable connections you've made. Were they based on a simple exchange of business cards, or were they nurtured over shared lunches, coffee chats, or project collaborations? The chances are that the latter resonates more. Because when connections are built on mutual respect, trust, and understanding, they tend to last.

The beauty of genuine networking is that professional environments do not bind it. It can happen anywhere - on a train, at a bookstore, during a hobby class, at a school function, or even on a hiking trail. When we open ourselves up to the world, ready to listen and share, we attract deep and meaningful connections.

Genuine networking is a two-way street. It's not about what you can get, but what you can give. Maybe it's a piece of advice, a book recommendation, a contact, or simply your time and empathy. We sow the seeds of solid and reciprocal relationships when approaching networking with a giving mindset.

It's also essential to understand that networking is a continual process. It's not a one-off event, but a journey. Relationships need to be nurtured, just like plants. They need time, care, understanding, and sometimes, even patience.

Now, you may ask, in an increasingly digital world where face-to-face interactions are becoming rare, how do we network genuinely? The medium may have changed, but the essence remains the same. Be genuine whether you're conversing over a video call, an email, or a social media platform. Share your stories, ask questions, show interest, and, most importantly, listen. In the digital age, the power of attentive listening cannot be emphasized enough.

Lastly, as you navigate the world of networking, remember to stay true to yourself. Authenticity is your most significant asset. People connect with real emotions, real stories, and authentic experiences. So, be yourself whether you're at a community gathering or a social networking platform. Share your journey, your dreams, your failures, and your learnings. Because that's what networking is all about - connecting, growing, and evolving together.

Networking is much more than the buzzword it's often made out to be. It's an art, a journey, and a celebration of human connection. So, the next time you find yourself in a networking situation, take a deep breath, let go of expectations, and dive deep into the world of stories, experiences, and genuine connections. Ultimately, it's not about how many contacts you have but the depth and quality of the relationships you've nurtured.

Building Authentic Connections

In a time when social media and quick texting are prevalent, genuinely connecting with another individual must be understood in translation. The sheer volume of our digital interactions sometimes overshadows the quality of our real-life connections. But now, more than ever, there's a growing hunger for authenticity in our interactions, a desire to peel back the layers of superficiality and truly connect, heart to heart, soul to soul.

Let's start with a reflection. Think about the last time you felt genuinely connected to someone. It could have been a heartfelt conversation with a friend, a moment of shared laughter with a colleague, or even an exchange of understanding glances with a stranger on the train. These moments of genuine connection resonate deeply within us and remind us of our inherent human need to belong, be understood, and be seen for who we are.

But what does it mean to connect authentically? And more importantly, how can we cultivate such connections in our daily lives?

Deep Listening

The art of listening seems straightforward, but genuine listening goes beyond merely hearing words. It involves tuning into the emotions, body language, and the unsaid. When we listen deeply, we offer the other person a safe space to express themselves freely. This form of active listening lays the foundation for authentic connection, where we're present in the moment, not just waiting for our turn to speak.

Being Vulnerable

While vulnerability might seem like a sign of weakness to some, it's a testament to our courage. Sharing our fears, aspirations, mistakes, and experiences requires bravery. By opening up, we invite others to do the same, fostering an environment of trust and mutual respect. The most profound connections are often forged in this space of shared vulnerability.

Quality over Quantity

We spread ourselves thin in our quest to be everywhere, know everyone, and do everything. But authentic connections are rarely about numbers. It's better to have a few deep, meaningful relationships than numerous shallow ones. Investing time and energy in fewer relationships allows us to go beyond the surface and truly get to know the other person.

Empathy and Open-mindedness

We all come from different walks of life, each carrying our bag of experiences, beliefs, and perspectives. The authentic connection doesn't require us to agree on everything. Instead, it asks for empathy and an open mind. It's about understanding where the other person comes from, even if we don't necessarily align with their views.

Consistent Communication

Building and maintaining authentic connections requires effort and consistency. Regularly checking in with loved ones, friends, or colleagues—not out of obligation but genuine concern and interest—can go a long way. Small gestures, like a random text to see how someone's day was, can make a difference.

Shared Experiences

Engage in activities, whether hiking, cooking, sports, or even working on a project, which can enhance connection. Shared experiences give us memories to cherish and offer insights into the other person's world, their strengths, weaknesses, likes, and dislikes.

Setting Boundaries

To connect authentically, we sometimes need to set boundaries. It's essential to recognize when we need time for ourselves or when specific topics are off-limits. Healthy boundaries ensure that our connections remain respectful and mutual.

Staying True to Yourself

The most authentic connections stem from being genuine. Pretending to be someone we're not, or trying too hard to fit into a mold, can be emotionally exhausting and rarely leads to real relationships. By embracing our authentic selves, quirks, and all, we attract connections that resonate on the same frequency.

In a world that often feels disconnected despite the never-ending ways to 'connect,' seeking and building authentic relationships is comforting for our souls. As we navigate through life's intricacies, these genuine connections become our anchors, providing comfort, understanding, and an assurance that amidst the vastness of the universe, there's someone who truly 'gets' us.

So, the next time you meet someone new or even reconnect with an old acquaintance, take a moment to delve deeper, listen a little more intently, and share more of your true self. You'll find the essence of human connection in these authentic exchanges.

Nurturing Your Network

In the modern age, "It's not what you know, but who you know" seems more pertinent than ever. At the heart of this saying lies a profound truth about the power of human connections and the importance of nurturing our network. It's about forging meaningful relationships based on mutual respect, understanding, and genuine interest.

How do you cultivate and nurture quality connections?

Authenticity is Key

Genuine interest can't be faked. When you reach out to someone for advice or to get to know them better, come from a place of authenticity. Remember, people can sense insincerity. Instead of approaching networking as a transaction, view it as a chance to learn and grow. It's this authentic curiosity that forms the foundation of lasting connections.

Less Can Mean More

It's tempting to get caught in the numbers game, especially in the age of social media, where the number of followers or connections often equates to influence. However, when nurturing your network, depth is more vital than breadth. Investing time and energy in deepening a few critical relationships can be far more rewarding than having many superficial acquaintances.

Reciprocity Matters

Networking is a two-way street. While seeking help or advice is natural, it's equally important to offer value in return. Whether sharing a relevant article, making an introduction, or providing feedback, ensure you're also giving back to your network. This reciprocity is what keeps the relationship dynamic and mutually beneficial.

Stay Updated

Life is ever evolving. People change jobs, change schools, move cities, or dive into new ventures. Make an effort to stay updated about significant events or changes in the lives of your connections. A simple congratulatory message about a new job or checking in during life transitions can reinforce your bond.

Regular Check-ins

You don't always need a reason to reconnect. Sometimes, a simple 'thinking of you' message or a quick call to catch up can work wonders in keeping the relationship alive. Without any immediate agenda, these random check-ins emphasize you value the relationship beyond mere professional interests.

Engage in Meaningful Conversations

Move beyond the small talk. Engage in deeper, more meaningful conversations. Discuss industry trends, share books or articles you've recently read, or explore mutual interests. These in-depth interactions not only enrich your knowledge but also strengthen your bond.

Attend Public Events

While digital communication tools have made staying in touch easier, nothing beats face-to-face interactions. Whenever possible, attend in-person events. These gatherings are a chance to make new friends who have shared interests.

Be a Connector

Act as a bridge between your connections. If you know two people in your network who can benefit from getting to know each other, introduce them. Playing the role of a connector enhances your value in the network and strengthens the web of connections around you.

Offer Help Before Asking

Before you reach out with a request, ask yourself if you've recently offered assistance or value to that connection. Leading with value or help makes it easier for the other person to reciprocate when you need assistance.

Celebrate Successes

Be it a graduation, a birthday, a new adventure, or personal milestones like weddings or anniversaries–celebrate your connections' successes and joyous occasions. It shows that you genuinely care about their well-being and success.

Seek Feedback and Advice

Be open to feedback. Contact trusted individuals in your network for advice or feedback on your ideas. It gives you fresh perspectives and involves them in your journey, creating a deeper bond with your peers.

Chapter 15

On a chilly Saturday morning in the heart of the city, the park at Maple Square bustled with activity. Residents gathered, holding brooms and rakes, with one mission in mind: reclaiming their garden from neglect. This event was the brainchild of Ava, a 16-year-old resident of Maple Square, who felt the park had seen better days and decided to do something about it.

Ava's journey began a month prior when she noticed the park's deteriorating condition. The once green haven was now marred by litter, graffiti, and overgrown grass. Memories of her childhood, playing amidst laughter and blooming flowers, contrasted sharply with its present state. Instead of just reminiscing, Ava chose to act. She contacted her neighbors, used social media, and even spoke at a local council meeting, mobilizing everyone for a park cleanup day.

What transpired that Saturday morning wasn't just the physical restoration of a park. It was the revival of community spirit. Neighbors who had been mere strangers started conversing, children got lessons in responsibility, and elders shared stories of the park's golden days. By evening, Maple Square Park was transformed, not only in appearance but in essence.

Ava's effort in Maple Square is a testament to the profound impact of civic engagement. The term 'civic engagement' often conjures images of voting booths or political rallies. However, at its core, civic engagement encapsulates every action an individual takes to make a difference in their community. And its value? Far-reaching and transformative.

The beauty of civic engagement lies in its ability to empower individuals. Every voice matters; every hand counts. When Ava took up the cause of reviving the park, she wasn't an elected official or a community leader; she was a concerned citizen. Her story dispels the myth that one needs power or position to make a change. All it requires is initiative and conviction.

Such individual actions serve as a catalyst, inspiring others to act. When one stands up for a cause, it ripples across the community, awakening others. The spirit of 'doing' becomes contagious. What starts as an individual's endeavor soon snowballs into a collective mission. The park cleanup wasn't just Ava's project; it became a community's shared vision.

Civic engagement strengthens the social fabric. In a world increasingly fragmented by virtual interactions, such endeavors provide an opportunity for genuine human connection. On that day, Maple Square didn't just witness the restoration of a park; it experienced the mending of broken bonds and the forging of new ones.

The benefits also transcend the immediate. Engaged citizens foster accountable governments. When individuals like Ava voice concerns, ask questions, and demand action, it keeps those in power on their toes, ensuring that they prioritize public welfare. By actively participating in community matters, citizens gain a deeper understanding of governance and policymaking, enabling informed decisions during elections.

Additionally, civic engagement acts as a beacon for future generations. Seeing Ava's leadership, younger residents of Maple Square are likely to grow up with an ingrained sense of responsibility towards their community. They learn that change isn't just about grand gestures but consistent small actions. As they say, 'change begins at home,' what better place to start than one's community?

As dusk settled on Maple Square and residents headed home, they left with more than just the satisfaction of a well-done day. They carried a renewed sense of purpose and the knowledge that their efforts had more significance. The park became a symbol of what's possible when a community comes together, led by the spirit of civic engagement.

For cities and towns everywhere, Maple Square stands as a reminder. A reminder that every individual possesses the power to effect change, that civic duty goes beyond just casting a vote, and that when people engage with their surroundings, magic unfolds.

Stories like Ava's offer hope in an era often characterized by individualism and indifference. They reaffirm the belief that individuals, when engaged, can shape communities and that every action, no matter how small, has value. The echoes of that chilly Saturday morning in Maple Square will reverberate for years, inspiring countless Avas to take the reins and make a difference. And in these ripples lies the true essence and value of civic engagement.

Making a Difference Locally

With her worn-out sneakers and a heart full of ambition, Evelyn walked the cobbled streets of Rosewood, her small hometown nestled between hills and history. For most, Rosewood was a forgotten relic, where time moved slowly, and change seemed even slower. But for Evelyn, this quaint town was a canvas waiting for strokes of innovation.

Growing up, she had heard tales of the town's golden era. The old-timers spoke of bustling marketplaces, lively festivals, and an infectious community spirit. But now, Rosewood seemed to have lost its luster, with shuttered shops, vacant parks, and a younger generation eager to move to the city's bright lights.

Yet, Evelyn saw potential where others saw stagnation. She believed that significant changes could happen even in the smallest of places. And more importantly, these changes didn't always need massive funding or government intervention. Sometimes, it took a little initiative, community spirit, and the belief that local actions could significantly impact.

One summer evening, Evelyn gathered a few like-minded friends on her porch. Together, they brainstormed ways to infuse life back into Rosewood. They realized the town's strength was its close-knit community. While they didn't have the resources of a big city, they had something even more potent: the power of collective action.

Their first endeavor was to revive the local marketplace. It wasn't just about commerce; it was about restoring the heart of Rosewood. They contacted local artisans, farmers, and craftsmen, organizing a weekly farmer's market. A location where one can purchase fresh food yet an event, complete with live music, art displays, and food stalls.

The response was overwhelming. Residents, who once drove miles to a supermarket, now looked forward to the weekly market. It became a melting pot of conversations, laughter, and shared stories. Children learned the joys of fresh farm produce while older people reconnected with the flavors of their youth.

Emboldened by the marketplace's success, Evelyn and her team took on more projects. They transformed the town's derelict park into a community garden. Residents could rent plots, growing their vegetables and flowers. This garden became more than just a place to plant seeds; it fostered relationships. Neighbors collaborated, exchanging gardening tips and celebrating bountiful harvests.

Then there was the community library, operating from a refurbished bus. Residents donated books, and every weekend, the bus would park in different parts of town, its shelves open to eager readers. Storytelling sessions, book clubs, and author meets made literature accessible and fun.

As months turned into years, Rosewood began to change. The town that once seemed on the brink of oblivion was buzzing with activity. But it wasn't just about events or projects. It was about a renewed sense of pride, identity, and belonging.

People who had once thought of leaving started investing in their hometowns. A local café opened up, hosting poetry slams and open mic nights. Teenagers started a digital project documenting Rosewood's history, ensuring that future generations knew their roots.

The transformation of Rosewood is a testament to the incredible power of local actions. Evelyn and her team didn't set out to change the world. They aimed to make a difference in their corner of it. And in doing so, they ignited a spark illuminating an entire community.

The story of Rosewood is not unique. Across the world, in big and small towns, individuals realize that waiting for sweeping changes often leads to disappointment. Instead, local, grassroots initiatives driven by passionate citizens can bring about the transformation they seek.

For those looking to make a difference, the first step is to observe, listen, and understand the unique needs of their community. Every place has strengths and challenges, and solutions must be tailor made. It's also crucial to remember that change doesn't happen overnight. There will be setbacks, naysayers, and moments of doubt. But as Rosewood showed, persistence pays off.

Ultimately, it's not about how big an action is, but how deep its impact runs. Small initiatives include a revived marketplace, a community garden, or a mobile library. But for the residents of Rosewood, these weren't just projects; they were lifelines, rekindling hope and forging connections.

Rosewood is a beacon of hope in today's complex world, where issues often seem insurmountable. It reminds us that change starts at home, in our neighborhoods, towns, and communities. And when individuals like Evelyn take the lead, even the sleepiest of towns can awaken to a bright, vibrant tomorrow. Making a difference locally isn't just about improving a particular place; it's about uplifting its people, one small action at a time.

Global Citizenship

In the heart of bustling New York City, Arjun often paused, closed his eyes, and reminisced about his childhood in Mumbai. The distant chants of street vendors, the aroma of spicy street food, and the constant hum of a city that never sleeps. It was a stark contrast to his current life, surrounded by skyscrapers amidst the orchestrated chaos of Times Square. Yet, he felt deeply connected to both worlds, a bridge spanning the East and the West.

Being a global citizen, as Arjun often referred to himself, wasn't just about living in different parts of the world. It was a mindset, a way of embracing the diversity of human experiences and weaving oneself into them. It was about understanding that our world is vast yet interconnected, and every individual action could ripple across borders, affecting communities miles away.

As a child, Arjun had learned to value the principles of unity in diversity. His parents, deeply rooted in Indian traditions, had always been keen on exposing him to global perspectives. They hosted exchange students, subscribed to international magazines, and ensured that family vacations were about leisure and learning from different cultures. This early exposure had sown the seeds of curiosity in Arjun. He wanted to explore, understand, and immerse himself in the myriad cultures that painted the world's canvas.

His chance came when he received a scholarship for undergraduate studies in New York. Leaving the shores of Mumbai was bittersweet. He was stepping out of his comfort zone, leaving behind familiar sights and sounds. But the world beckoned, and Arjun was ready.

Life in New York was a whirlwind. Arjun's journey was symbolic of every international student, from the initial days of homesickness to gradually finding his footing. He learned to appreciate the nuances of American culture, from its emphasis on individualism to its entrepreneurial spirit. He made friends from across the globe, each a window to a different world, each story adding a thread to his evolving identity as a global citizen.

But being a global citizen was not just about embracing different cultures. It was also about recognizing the challenges our world faced and playing an active role in addressing them. Arjun realized this when he volunteered for a sustainable farming project in Ghana during a summer break. The experience was transformative. He witnessed firsthand the struggles of local farmers battling the effects of climate change and economic disparities. It was here that Arjun understood that global citizenship meant responsibility. A responsibility to contribute positively, to be aware, and to leverage one's privilege to make a difference.

Upon returning to New York, Arjun became an advocate for sustainable practices. He organized workshops, collaborated with NGOs, and used his unique position as a bridge between the East and the West to foster dialogues. He realized that every individual could make a difference, and in today's interconnected world, even the most minor action in one corner could have profound effects on another.

Years rolled by, and Arjun transitioned from a student to a professional working in a multinational company. His role required him to travel, and each destination was an opportunity to further his journey as a global citizen. From understanding the Japanese's meticulous precision to appreciating Brazilians' vibrant community spirit, Arjun's world expanded, and so did his sense of responsibility.

He spearheaded corporate initiatives prioritizing sustainability, championed diversity, and promoted cross-cultural exchanges. But beyond the boardroom, Arjun continued his journey, learning languages, sampling cuisines, and forging friendships that spanned continents.

Reflecting on his journey, Arjun realized that being a global citizen was both a privilege and a commitment. It was about celebrating differences while recognizing our shared humanity. It was about understanding that the path to harmony lay in mutual respect, understanding, and cooperation in a world full of divisions.

Arjun's story is a testament to the potential within each of us to be global citizens. In an age where information is at our fingertips, borders are blurring, and cultures are intertwining, Global citizenship is now required, not an option. It's about broadening horizons, fostering empathy, and understanding that our actions, no matter how small, have global implications.

Ultimately, being a global citizen is a journey of discovery, growth, and responsibility. It's about recognizing that our world is a beautiful mosaic of experiences, and each of us has a role to play in preserving and enriching it, just like Arjun, who, from the bylines of Mumbai to the avenues of New York, found his purpose and his home, as a citizen of the world.

Chapter 16

I n a world filled with so many things vying for our attention, time has become the most coveted treasure. How many times have you wished for more hours in the day? How often have you mourned over lost time or yearned for a moment of pause? Unlock a world of productivity and accomplishment by learning how to prioritize your time.

Imagine a jar filled with sand, pebbles, and large rocks. If you start with the sand, you'll need more room for the rocks. But everything fits if you begin with the big rocks and then fill them in with pebbles and sand. The same goes for life. If we drown in the minutiae, we risk never addressing our most significant commitments and passions. The big rocks represent those essential, high-priority tasks, while the sand is the small stuff that can wait.

The first step to adequate time prioritization is understanding your 'big rocks.' These could be long-term goals like writing a book, short-term tasks like finding a new job, or personal commitments like spending more quality time with family. Once identified, these take precedence.

Now, the question arises: How does one sift through the big and small tasks and align them with the compass of priorities?

The key lies in self-awareness and strategic planning.

Reflection and Recognition

Begin by reflecting on your personal and professional goals. What do you wish to achieve in the next week, month, or year? Recognizing these goals will give you a clearer picture of where your time should be spent. It's easy to be deceived by illusions of busyness, mistaking it for productivity. But once you've laid out your primary objectives, it becomes simpler to weed out the redundant tasks.

Learn to Say No

This might be the oldest technique in the book, but it remains one of the most effective. Time is finite, and every 'yes' is a 'no' to something else. By being selective about commitments, you safeguard your time for what aligns with your goals and values.

One of the most empowering yet challenging skills is the ability to say 'no.' It's tempting to take on every opportunity, attend every gathering, or accept every invitation that comes your way. However, stretching oneself too thin can lead to burnout and sub-par results. Prioritizing your time means protecting it, and sometimes that requires turning down opportunities or engagements that don't align with your primary goals.

The Power of Delegation

Remember, prioritizing your time doesn't mean doing everything yourself. Understand the power of delegation. Trust in the abilities of others and hand over tasks that they can handle, freeing up your time for more critical studies.

Utilize Technology

We live in the digital age, where technology can become a colossal distraction or a potent tool for time management. Use apps and software designed for task management, reminders, and scheduling. But beware of the rabbit hole of notifications and constant checking.

Time Blocking

Set aside distinct periods for various activities. For instance, reserve the first two hours of your workday for uninterrupted, focused work. Time blocking helps ensure that each task gets its due time and that you're not just firefighting urgent matters all day.

Regularly Re-Evaluate

Priorities change. What seemed essential last month might not hold the same weight now. Regularly review your goals and task list. This re-evaluation ensures that you're always aligned with your most pressing priorities.

Mindful Living

While the mechanics of time prioritization are crucial, so is the spirit with which you approach time. Understand that time is a finite resource that flows regardless of our control. Being present at the moment, savoring experiences, and practicing mindfulness add quality to the time spent.

In conclusion, mastering the art of time prioritization is a journey, not a destination. It's a continuous process of learning, adjusting, and refining. But at its core, it's about making deliberate decisions that fit your values and ambitions. As you tread this path, remember Lao Tzu once said, "Time is a manufactured thing. I don't have time is the equivalent of I don't want to." Embrace the opportunity to prioritize your time whenever possible.

Tools and Techniques for Effective Time Management

Time is an elusive concept. It races during our best moments and seems to stand still during the toughest. And while we can't control its passage, we can certainly control how we navigate it. Mastering time management isn't just about getting more tasks done; it's about ensuring that our days resonate with purpose, productivity, and some well-deserved peace.

From ancient sundials to today's sophisticated digital calendars, humanity has been obsessed with measuring and managing time. As our lives have become more complex, so has our need to harness time so that it becomes an ally rather than an adversary.

So, how do we tame this wild horse called time? Combining tried-and-true techniques with a pinch of modern technology, we can create a harmonious rhythm in our daily lives.

The Pomodoro Technique

Inspired by a tomato-shaped kitchen timer, the Pomodoro Technique breaks work into intervals, usually 25 minutes long, followed by a 5-minute break. This encourages intense focus and productivity, followed by a short rest period, revitalizing the mind. Every fourth break is about 15 minutes longer to ensure our brain gets its due rest.

The Time Audit

You must know where it's going before you can manage your time effectively. Spend a week logging everything you do down to the minute. At the end of the week, analyze your activities. You may discover you need to spend more time on tasks that are neither urgent nor important or get sidetracked by frequent interruptions.

A Two-Minute limit

Do it right away if it takes up to two minutes. Simple but powerful. By immediately tackling tasks that require minimal time, you can clear minor chores off your to-do list and focus on more significant projects.

Organize comparable jobs into groups and complete them all at once. For instance, if you have multiple emails, writing and sending them in one batch is more efficient than having them scattered throughout the day. This way, your mind stays in one "mode" of operation, reducing the mental load of constantly switching tasks.

Eisenhower Matrix

This is the art of decision-making. The matrix classifies tasks into four categories: Urgent and Important, Not Urgent but Important, Urgent but Not Important, and neither Urgent nor Important. This visualization helps to realign our efforts and attention to what truly matters. Organizing tasks into categories helps you to decide what needs to be done immediately, when they should be completed, who will do them, and even which ones can be dropped altogether.

Digital Calendars and Task Managers

In our connected age, digital tools like Google Calendar, Trello, or Asana can streamline task lists, set reminders, and even allow collaborative projects to be managed with ease. With these tools, everything you need is in one place, accessible from any device, anytime.

The 80/20 Rule

The Pareto Principle, as it is also known, states that 80% of results come from 20% of efforts. We can achieve more in less time by identifying and focusing on the crucial 20% of tasks that yield the most significant results.

Limit Multitasking

It might feel productive to juggle multiple tasks simultaneously, but studies have shown that our brains aren't wired for it. Instead, we're merely switching rapidly between jobs, which can drain mental energy and reduce efficiency. Focus on one task, see it through, and then move on to the next.

Time Blocking

Allocate blocks of uninterrupted time for specific activities. By segmenting your day into clearly defined chunks of time for particular tasks or types of work, you ensure that essential jobs get their dedicated attention and reduce the inertia of starting a scheme.

Mindful Pause

Amid the hustle and bustle, taking moments of pause is essential. These moments aren't about idleness, but about clarity. They provide a bird's-eye view, a moment to reassess, recalibrate, and move forward with renewed focus.

Time management is a mix of discipline and flexibility. While tools and techniques provide the framework, intuition, and self-awareness, infuse it with life. Remember, the goal isn't to pack our days with countless tasks but to find harmony, purpose, and joy in the journey.

The Importance of Breaks and Downtime

In the rapid pace of today's world, every moment is accounted for, and every second is valuable. We live by alarms, planners, and calendars, trying to squeeze productivity out of every minute. But amidst this hustle, many overlook a hidden gem: the art and importance of breaks and downtime.

Picture this. You're reading an intense novel full of plot twists and high drama. If that tension continued unabated from cover to cover, you'd likely feel drained, overwhelmed, and in need of a quiet moment by the end of the book. The same holds true for our lives. Without pauses and breaks, the narrative of our daily existence becomes a relentless tension that can wear us down.

But what is it about breaks and downtime that makes them so vital?

First and foremost, breaks allow our minds to rest and reset. Just like an athlete wouldn't train continuously without risking injury, our brains need rest intervals to function optimally. Constant work, be it physical or mental, leads to diminishing returns. After a certain point, you're no longer at your best, and the quality of your output begins to suffer. Pausing for a brief moment, even to take a deep breath or gaze out of the window, can provide that much-needed reset, allowing you to return to your task with renewed vigor.

Downtime is often when our best ideas surface. When we step away from a task, our subconscious mind continues to work on the problem. This is why many epiphanies occur during showers, walks, or even dreams. Permitting ourselves to step back can lead to unexpected and innovative solutions that might not arise under continuous work pressure.

Downtime also offers an opportunity for reflection. In goal-oriented lives, we're often so focused on the destination that we forget to enjoy the journey. Pauses provide a moment to take stock, look around, appreciate where we are, and recalibrate if needed. Without these reflective moments, life becomes a blur of tasks lacking meaning and purpose.

Emotionally, breaks act as a buffer, protecting us from the ill effects of chronic stress and burnout. Continuous engagement, especially in high-pressure scenarios, can elevate stress hormones like cortisol in our bodies. This could eventually result in several health problems, from insomnia and anxiety to cardiovascular issues. Breaks, even short ones, can counteract these effects, giving our body and mind a momentary respite.

Physically, our eyes demand downtime, especially in today's screen-dominated world. The 20-20-20 rule advises looking for 20 seconds every 20 minutes while gazing at anything 20 feet away, which is a testament to giving our eyes a break. This lowers the possibility of eyestrain and other related issues.

And then there's the sheer joy of leisure—moments where we do things not for productivity or achievement but for the pure love of the activity. Whether reading a book, playing an instrument, watching a movie, or engaging in any other hobby, these moments of downtime enrich our lives. They provide a counterbalance, a reminder that while work and achievement are essential, so are joy, passion, and play.

But how can we integrate breaks effectively into our lives? It's more straightforward than it seems.

Prioritize them: Understand and internalize their importance. They're not wasted moments; they're essential for holistic well-being.

Schedule them: If you have a packed day, schedule short breaks just as you would meetings or tasks.

Diversify your breaks: Every pause can be different. Mix up physical activity with relaxation. A short walk can be as rejuvenating as a ten-minute meditation.

Disconnect: If possible, step away from screens. The digital world is relentless, and a proper break often means disconnecting, even if momentarily.

Be present: Use breaks as an opportunity to practice mindfulness. Be fully in that moment, whether you're sipping tea or gazing at the clouds.

In conclusion, breaks and downtime are not luxuries; they're necessities. They are the quiet yet essential intervals in the symphony of our lives, giving depth, richness, and harmony to our days. So, the next time you find yourself drowning in tasks, remember the rejuvenating power of pauses. Embrace them, cherish them, and let them elevate your life's melody to new, soulful heights.

Chapter 17

M yrna lived in a quaint town nestled amidst rolling hills and lush forests. Myrna wasn't a yogi, psychologist, or spiritual guru. She was an ordinary woman with a simple life but harbored an extraordinary understanding of life's most intricate triad: the connection between the mind, body, and spirit.

The townspeople often remarked on Myrna's radiant energy. Despite life's ups and downs, she seemed to float gracefully through challenges, constantly becoming more muscular and centered. Many approached her, curious about the secret to her serenity.

"It's quite simple," Myrna would often begin, her eyes twinkling with a certain wisdom. "Understanding and nurturing the connection between our mind, body, and spirit."

The mind was the grand storyteller for Myrna, weaving narratives that could elevate and limit us. Our thoughts held immense power, shaping our perceptions, actions, and, ultimately, our realities. Positive reviews could invigorate us, while negative ones could trap us in cycles of doubt and desolation.

On a summer day, a young man named Leon approached Myrna when the sun painted golden streaks across the sky. He felt trapped in a maze of anxiety, unable to escape the weight of his thoughts. Myrna, listening intently, told him to observe his thoughts without judgment. "Imagine you're by a riverbank," she suggested, "and your thoughts are the flowing water. Don't try to change their course. Just watch them." Over time, this mindfulness practice helped Leon gain clarity and perspective, allowing him to navigate his anxieties more effectively.

Yet, Myrna quickly noted that while the mind was powerful, it wasn't standalone. The body, she believed, was the vessel through which the reason expressed itself. Every thought triggered a physiological response. Stress, for instance, wasn't just a mental state; it manifested in tense shoulders, a clenched jaw, or a racing heart.

Ella, a dancer in the town, once confided in Myrna about her creative block. While she was mentally motivated, her body felt lethargic. Myrna introduced her to holistic health–nourishing the body with wholesome foods, engaging in regular physical activity, and listening to its subtle cues. Under Myrna's guidance, Ella began to practice yoga, focusing on aligning her breath with her movements. The synergy of breath and motion unlocked her physical vitality, and soon Ella's dance reflected a newfound fluidity and grace.

However, the triad would only be complete with the spirit. To Myrna, the heart was the silent observer, the eternal flame of consciousness. It was the essence of who we were beyond our mental narratives and physical realities. Tapping into this spirit was the key to holistic wellness.

An older woman, Patty, often felt a void despite her accomplishments and family. She sought Myrna's insight, yearning to fill her inside emptiness. Myrna spoke to her about meditation and the art of inner stillness. "In the silence," Myrna whispered, "you'll find your spirit's voice." Patty began to meditate, and she experienced moments of profound peace and interconnectedness over time. She realized that her spirit was not isolated but part of a vast cosmic dance.

Myrna's understanding of the mind-body-spirit connection was derived from something other than textbooks. It culminated from her life experiences, observations, and innate wisdom. She believed that each aspect of the triad influenced the other, and by harmonizing them, one could attain holistic well-being.

Myrna's insights permeated the town's consciousness as the years rolled by. People began to introspect deeply, care for their bodies more diligently, and seek spiritual solace. The morning saw townsfolk practicing mindfulness, afternoons echoed with the rhythmic cadence of breathing exercises, and the soft glow of meditation illuminated nights.

Myrna's legacy was not just her teachings, but the transformation she inspired. Through her, the town realized that well-being was not linear. It was a harmonious melody, a delicate dance of the mind, body, and spirit. Understanding and nurturing this connection, they discovered the path to true contentment and vitality.

And so, nestled amidst nature's bounty, the town became a beacon of holistic wellness, a testament to the timeless wisdom of the mind-body-spirit connection and the profound tranquility it could usher in.

Establishing a Routine for Holistic Health

There was a sanctuary in the heart of the bustling city of Libreville. Not a physical place but a realm of harmony, existing amid daily chaos. This realm was the world of Charmain, a woman known for her ethereal aura and tenacious spirit. Charmain wasn't a doctor, nor was she a spiritual healer. She was a librarian with a profound understanding of holistic health.

Now, what is a librarian's association with holistic health? The narrative starts on a soggy afternoon when a distressed young writer named Byron enters the library. He was battling writer's block, fatigue, and overwhelming existential angst. Spotting Charmain's calm demeanor, he approached her.

Sipping on her chamomile tea, Charmain began sharing her philosophy. "Our well-being is like a fabric made of many delicate threads," she began. "Each strand represents an aspect of our health—mental, physical, emotional, and spiritual. These all tie together, creating an intricate web of influence."

Byron listened, his intrigue deepening. Charmain then spoke about her daily routine, a melodic blend of activities that nourished each dimension of her well-being.

Morning's Mental Clarity: Charmain began her day with a practice she called 'mindful awakening.' Instead of reaching for her phone or diving straight into the day's tasks, she'd spend a few moments absorbing the environment, listening to the birds, feeling the texture of her sheets, and observing her thoughts. This daily practice honed her mental agility and offered clarity.

Noon's Physical Vitality: Afternoons were dedicated to her physical well-being. Charmain believed in the philosophy of 'movement as medicine.' She didn't restrict herself to a specific exercise regimen. Some days, she'd dance wildly to her favorite tunes; on others, she'd take long walks or practice yoga. The essence was to keep the body active, allowing energy to flow freely.

Evening's Emotional Reflection: Evenings were a time of emotional reflection. Charmain would write in her journal, not just about the day's events, but about her feelings. She'd express gratitude, process challenges, and visualize her aspirations. This emotional unloading kept her grounded, ensuring that pent-up emotions didn't cloud her inner peace.

Night's Spiritual Serenity: As the world slept, Charmain delved into her spiritual self. She meditated, but not in the conventional sense. She would sit by her window, gaze at the stars, and let her consciousness expand. She felt interconnected with the universe, a tiny yet integral part of the cosmic dance.

Charmain's routine was flexible. It wasn't about rigidly checking off activities from a list but ensuring each dimension of her well-being was catered to daily.

Inspired, Byron decided to create a routine tailored to his needs. He began waking up to the soft strumming of his guitar, channeling morning freshness into music. His afternoons were filled with short story writing, stimulating his mental faculties. By evening, he'd head to the local park, soaking in nature and reading a book. A therapeutic exercise catered to his emotional side. And nights? They became a realm of introspection, where he'd pen down his philosophical musings.

Weeks turned into months, and Byron's transformation was substantial. His writing bloomed, reflecting his newfound balance. Once a refuge from his challenges, the library became a sanctuary of shared wisdom.

More Libreville residents sought her counsel as word spread about Charmain's philosophy. They realized that holistic health wasn't a distant concept but a tangible, daily practice. Each person's routine differed, reflecting individual needs and preferences, but the essence remained, catering to the mental, physical, emotional, and spiritual.

Today, Libreville isn't just known for its skyscrapers and busy streets. It's known as the city of balance, where residents thrive harmoniously. Children are taught the significance of holistic health from a young age, offices have spaces for meditation, and parks resonate with collective yoga sessions.

And at the heart of it is a simple library and its librarian, Charmain. Through her wisdom, she offered books and pathways to well-being. Her legacy reminds us that holistic health isn't an abstract goal; it's a daily melody, a symphony of wholeness that we can compose with a bit of mindfulness and intention.

Seeking Support When Needed

Just as the sun started to set below the horizon, Elara found herself wandering the cobblestone streets of the old town. The weight of the world seemed to press down on her shoulders, with every step echoing the heaviness of her heart. Alone with her thoughts, the chaos of the day's trials and tribulations reverberated in her mind, making each breath feel laborious.

But amidst the busyness of her thoughts, there was a voice—a memory of her grandmother's words: "There's strength in seeking help, my dear. Remember, even the mightiest trees need the soil to hold them."

Growing up, Elara was always the pillar of strength for her family and friends. From solving disputes among her siblings to offering a listening ear to a friend in distress, she was the go-to person for everyone. This role became so ingrained in her identity that she forgot, or perhaps neglected, that even pillars need a foundation.

As she continued her aimless journey through the old town, she stumbled upon a quaint little café named 'Soulful Soups.' She entered, drawn by its warm lights and the melodic tunes floating through its open doors.

Inside, the café was filled with various people, each engrossed in their conversations. However, what caught her eye was a unique corner labeled 'Heart-to-Heart.' Here, strangers sat across from each other, sharing stories, laughter, and sometimes, tears.

Curious, Elara approached the corner and was soon greeted by an elderly gentleman named Mario. With twinkling eyes and a kind smile, he introduced himself as a retired therapist who now volunteered at the café, offering an open heart and listening ear to anyone in need.

Taking a seat, Elara began sharing her tale—of the burdens she carried, the expectations she felt weighed down by, and the loneliness that came from always being the strong one. As she spoke, Mario listened intently, his presence creating a cocoon of warmth and understanding around her.

When she finished, Mario spoke, his words flowing like a gentle stream. "Elara," he began, "Life has a way of making us wear masks. Over time, we become so accustomed to them we forget our true faces. But no matter how strong the appearance, everyone, at some point, needs a hand to hold."

He went on to share stories of his journey, of times when he, too, felt overwhelmed and sought support, emphasizing that it was during these moments of vulnerability that he discovered his true strength.

As the night deepened, the café began to empty, leaving the two enveloped in their shared vulnerability and newfound connection. When it was time to leave, Mario handed Elara a small notebook, its pages filled with tales of people who had sought solace in the 'Heart-to-Heart' corner, each a testament to the power of seeking help.

Elara left the café with a lighter heart and realized that strength didn't come from shouldering burdens alone but from the courage to admit when she got overwhelmed and needed support.

Months turned into years, and Elara was no longer the same. She became a beacon for others, reminding them of the strength of vulnerability and the importance of seeking support. She started community gatherings where people came together, not to celebrate their strengths but their moments of weakness, fostering a community bound by empathy and understanding.

And at the center of these gatherings was the notebook from 'Soulful Soups,' its pages filled with tales of resilience and the silent symphony of seeking support.

In today's world, where the narrative of individualism and self-reliance often overshadow the inherent human need for connection and support, Elara's journey serves as a poignant reminder. It tells us that it's okay to ask for help, that seeking support isn't a sign of weakness but of profound strength, and that we find our true essence in our moments of vulnerability.

So, the next time the world's weight feels like too much, remember Elara and her night at 'Soulful Soups.' Take off your mask, reach out, and embrace the beauty of human connection. In seeking support, we not only lighten our burdens, but also become a source of strength for others.

Chapter 18

In busy New York City, Anna's days were filled with meetings, buzzing smartphones, and the hypnotic rhythm of typing keyboards. She was the epitome of success - a young woman in her prime, ascending the corporate ladder with the ease of a seasoned mountaineer. Yet, as each day came to a close, a sense of hollowness would creep into her heart. The city lights that once dazzled her eyes now only seemed to mirror the emptiness she felt within.

On a particularly gloomy evening, as Anna strolled down the streets of Manhattan, she stood in front of 'Grace's,' an old bookshop she hadn't noticed before. Drawn in, she perused the aisles, and her eyes settled on a worn-out journal titled "The Chronicles of Generosity." Intrigued, she began reading the story of a man named Samuel.

Once a wealthy merchant, Samuel faced a series of misfortunes that dwindled his vast riches to nothing. But instead of bitterness, these trials brought about a transformation in him. He realized that while he had been wealthy in material possessions, he had been poor in spirit and kindness. Samuel then embarked on a journey across continents, offering his skills and labor, asking for nothing in return.

In an African village, he helped construct wells, bringing fresh water to those who had to walk miles to fetch it. In Asia, he taught children in makeshift schools under trees. In Europe, he assisted in rejuvenating post-war communities. But the most beautiful part of Samuel's story was his acts of service and the ripples they created.

The village with fresh water started a farming cooperative, the children he taught became educators and leaders in their communities, and the war-torn towns became bustling centers of art and culture. Samuel's acts of giving back had not just touched lives momentarily; they transformed entire communities for generations.

Anna was deeply moved. She realized that success wasn't just about personal gain, but was truly meaningful when it uplifted others. Inspired, she decided to start small. She used her corporate prowess to initiate a mentorship program in her company, guiding young talents who reminded her of herself when she first started. Weekends were dedicated to volunteering at local shelters or teaching financial literacy to underprivileged youth.

And the more she gave, the more she felt fulfilled. The void that once consumed her began to fill with heartwarming memories of gratitude-filled eyes and hopeful smiles. Anna became a beacon of inspiration in her circle. Colleagues joined her in her weekend ventures, friends initiated their community projects, and slowly, a movement of giving back began to ripple through the concrete jungle of New York.

One evening, as Anna sat on her apartment balcony overlooking the city, she realized that the dazzling lights of New York were no longer just reflections of its skyscrapers. They were echoes of generosity, of countless souls like her who had discovered the joy of giving back.

Years later, on a clear sunny day, 'Grace's' bookshop received a unique addition to its collection - a sequel to "The Chronicles of Generosity" penned by Anna herself. It narrated her journey from feeling lost in a metropolis to finding a purpose in giving. It was an ode to the silent symphony of generosity that resonates within every act of kindness, no matter how small.

Anna's story is a testament to the profound impact of giving back. It is not just about philanthropy or grand gestures. It's about recognizing that every individual, in their capacity, can make a difference. Whether offering a seat to an older adult on a bus, helping a colleague on a challenging project, or building wells in distant lands, every act of generosity sends ripples into the universe.

In giving, we receive. We are reminded of our interconnectedness and the shared human experience. It nurtures empathy, bridges divides, and fosters community spirit. It brings purpose to our lives, enriching our souls and uplifting those around us.

So, as you navigate life's journey amidst the hustle and challenges, take a moment to reflect on what you can give back. For in the echoes of generosity, you'll find the melodies of a life well-lived.

Finding Causes, You're Passionate About

When Sophie first walked through the urban streets of her city, she was, like many of us, a tad oblivious. The massive billboards advertising the latest tech gadgets, fragrances, and fashion trends captivated her attention. At its dizzying pace, the city was a constant stream of sensory overload, making it easy for her to overlook the subtle, underlying issues of urban life.

One winter evening, as Sophie was rushing home, she took a shortcut through a less frequented alleyway. There, she stumbled upon a sight that would forever change her perspective: a young girl, no older than ten, huddled in the cold, her eyes reflecting the world's weight.

In this poignant moment, she acted as a catalyst. The vastness of societal issues dawned on Sophie. From the children of the streets to the elderly struggling with loneliness, from the scars of environmental decay to the fight for rights and equality, the world was filled with causes waiting for champions.

But where does one start in a world that seems to be brimming with endless challenges?

Sophie began her journey of discovery by listening to her heart. She sought out stories not just from books or news articles but by speaking to individuals from various walks of life. The stories of struggles, hope, resilience, and dreams painted a clearer picture of where her passions indeed lay.

She met Rosa, a spirited environmentalist fighting to conserve local woodlands. Then there was Ahmed, who dedicated his life to uplifting the youth from gang violence. And Elina, a fervent advocate for mental health awareness. With each story, Sophie felt a resonance, a heartbeat of change echoing her own.

But during an art workshop organized for underprivileged children, Sophie's path became crystal clear. The sparkle in the kids' eyes as they poured their emotions onto canvas, the raw, unfiltered expression of their hopes, fears, dreams, and aspirations–it was here that Sophie realized her passion for harnessing the therapeutic power of art.

Starting small, she began organizing weekly art therapy sessions, using her modest apartment as a haven for these young souls. Word spread and the "Therapeutic Art" foundation was born soon. Through art, children were healing and finding their voices, turning their painful narratives into powerful messages of change.

Sophie's journey isn't unique. It's a testament to the age-old adage: where there's a will; there's a way. And the first step always begins with introspection.

In a world filled with endless causes, finding where one fits in can often feel overwhelming. Yet, each individual carries a unique blend of passion, skills, and experiences. It's a matter of tuning out the external noise and tuning into one's inner compass.

You might feel a pull towards animals and their well-being, or perhaps your heart aches at the thought of refugees in dire straits looking for a home. You may be passionate about ensuring education for all or championing the rights of marginalized communities. Every cause, big or small, has a ripple effect in the vast ocean of societal change.

Begin by asking yourself: What stirs your heart? What issues resonate deeply with you? Engaging in conversations, volunteering, attending seminars, or reading about global challenges. Often, the cause you're meant to champion is where your heart and mind align, pushing you to act, speak, and make a difference.

In this vast universe of causes, there's a particular corner waiting for you, a space that will amplify your voice, channel your efforts, and resonate with your heartbeat of change. And just like Sophie, you too will find that when passion meets purpose, transformation echoes are boundless.

Sustainable Philanthropy and Long-Term Impact

The sun was beginning to rise as Katiana, a dedicated philanthropist, walked through the small village of Taran, a community nestled in the heart of Africa. Children ran alongside her, their laughter echoing, filling the air with a joy that was both infectious and profound. But this scene of contentment was a far cry from what Taran looked like a decade ago.

Ten years prior, Taran had been on the brink of devastation. Droughts had decimated crops, and with most of the community dependent on farming, hunger loomed large. Aid organizations swooped in, providing immediate relief through food packages, bottled water, and clothing. However, within a few months, the aid dwindled, and Taran was left grappling with the same issues; their root causes still needed to be addressed.

Katiana's approach was different. She had a vision, not just of band-aid solutions, but of fostering a community that could thrive independently long after her involvement ended. This vision was rooted in the concept of sustainable philanthropy.

Rather than just providing fish, Katiana taught the villagers how to fish, metaphorically speaking. She introduced drought-resistant crops, spearheaded the creation of a water conservation system, and even set up workshops on modern farming techniques. They sent the village youth to neighboring towns for formal education, ensuring they could bring back a wealth of knowledge and innovative ideas.

As years went by, Taran began to transform. The once parched lands now bore lush crops. The educated and empowered youth started micro-businesses, from poultry farms to handicraft units, bringing economic stability. But what truly set Katiana's approach apart was her focus on empowering the community, especially women. Women were trained in skills like sewing and pottery, enabling them to contribute to the family's income.

Yet, Katiana's most remarkable achievement wasn't just the tangible development. It was the sense of ownership she instilled in the villagers. They were no longer passive recipients of aid, but active participants in their destinies. They took pride in their progress, ensuring every initiative, whether a new well or a school, was maintained with love and care.

Over time, Taran became a beacon, a shining example of what sustainable philanthropy can achieve. Neighboring villages began to take notice, adopting similar development models, setting off a ripple effect of positive change.

Sustainable philanthropy is more than just financial aid. It's about understanding the intricacies of the communities we wish to help. It's about respecting their culture, traditions, and aspirations while introducing them to tools and knowledge that can catalyze growth. It's an acknowledgment that while immediate aid is essential in crises, long-term impact requires patience, persistence, and a deep-seated belief in human potential.

Katiana often said, "When you plant a tree, you may never enjoy its shade or fruits. But somewhere down the line, a weary traveler or a hungry soul will. And that's the essence of true giving."

In today's world, where issues seem impossible and challenges are multifaceted, sustainable philanthropy offers a beacon of hope. It tells us that we can sow seeds of change that will flourish for generations with the right approach, dedication, and an understanding heart.

As we step into the future, let us remember the lessons from Taran and Katiana. Let us strive not just to give but to empower, not just to provide but to uplift, ensuring that our acts of philanthropy leave footprints of enduring, meaningful change. In this quest, every effort counts, every vision matters, and every heart that believes can make a world of difference.

Chapter 19

On a sunny afternoon along the Delaware River in Philadelphia, Michelle sat across from her old friend Sam, discussing their recent endeavors. Both had embarked on entrepreneurial journeys, yet their experiences were starkly different. Michelle's organic skincare line had skyrocketed in popularity, earning her a spot on a popular talk show. Sam, who had launched a tech startup, struggled to gain traction despite having a groundbreaking product.

As the conversation meandered, Michelle observed that startled Sam. "You know, it's not always about having the best product or idea. It's about how you present it and, more importantly, how you present yourself." That is the power and importance of personal branding.

In today's digital age, with countless individuals and businesses competing for attention, standing out isn't a luxury; it's a necessity. And personal branding is the beacon that can illuminate one's unique value proposition in an over-saturated market.

Imagine the global business landscape as a grand masquerade ball. Among the sea of masked faces, those without a distinct mask or persona are often overlooked, no matter how skilled or talented they are. Personal branding is that unique mask, a carefully crafted narrative that encapsulates who you are, what you stand for, and what sets you apart.

But why does this matter so much?

Trust in an Age of Skepticism

Consumers today are inundated with choices. From skincare to technology, numerous products and services are vying for their attention and trust. But trust doesn't come easily in an era of rampant scandals and fake news. Personal branding acts as a bridge, connecting the faceless entity of a business to a human, relatable persona. When consumers feel they know the person behind a brand, their trust comes more effortlessly, and their loyalty solidifies.

Positioning in a Sea of Similarity

How often have we come across products or services that seem indistinguishable? In such scenarios, it's the strength of personal branding that can tip the scales. A compelling personal brand can transform an ordinary product into an extraordinary experience. Think of Elon Musk and Tesla or Oprah and her media empire. Their private brands infuse their ventures with a unique flavor, setting them leagues apart from competitors.

Authentic Stories

Authenticity shines through in a world of curated social media highlights like a rare gem. Personal branding isn't about projecting a false image. Instead, it's about weaving genuine stories, experiences, and values into a cohesive narrative. This authenticity appeals to consumers and fosters deeper connections, turning customers into brand ambassadors.

Adaptability in Changing Times

Business strategies and products might evolve, but a solid personal brand remains a consistent anchor. It allows individuals and businesses to pivot, explore new avenues, and take risks while maintaining a loyal clientele invested in the brand's journey, not just its products.

Amplifying Opportunities

A robust personal brand can open doors one didn't even know existed. Whether speaking engagements, collaborations, investments, or media appearances, personal branding amplifies one's presence, making opportunities more accessible and abundant.

Sam had an epiphany as the afternoon sun began to dip, casting shadows on the flowing river. He realized that his groundbreaking tech product needed more than innovative features; it needed his story, passion, and unique perspective. Emboldened, he embarked on a journey of introspection, determined to craft a personal brand that resonated, captivated, and inspired.

The message is clear for all the Sams out there: In the grand theater of business and life, it's not just about the performance but also the persona. Personal branding is more than just a strategy; it's an art, a continuous journey of self-discovery and expression. And in this journey lies the power to transform, influence, and leave an indelible mark on the world. So, dive deep, embrace your narrative, and let your brand shine!

Building Your Online and Offline Brand

There's an old saying that when you enter a room, your reputation enters before you. In the age of digital ubiquity and globalization, this ring truer than ever, with a tiny twist: now, your reputation precedes you in both virtual rooms and physical spaces.

Selma, an ambitious young entrepreneur, unexpectedly learned this lesson. With dreams of launching her sustainable clothing line, she worked hard behind the scenes, crafting beautiful, eco-friendly designs. On the day she finally unveiled her brand, the audience's reaction was mixed, not because of the quality of her products but because of her brand's inconsistent presence.

On the internet, her brand flourished with eye-catching visuals, educational material, and avenues for conversation and interaction. But offline, her pop-up shop felt disconnected, with minimal branding elements, and needed to have the personality that her online space radiated.

Selma's experience underscores the essential lesson of the modern branding age: the harmonious integration of online and offline branding is not just beneficial—it's crucial.

Blending the Digital and Tangible

Consumers don't distinguish between online and offline experiences in our interconnected world—they weave them together. When consumers discover a brand on social media and walk into its physical store the next day, they expect a cohesive experience, a seamless transition from the digital world's pixels to the tactile world's textures.

Selma began her integration journey by first recognizing each realm's value to her brand.

The Digital Canvas

Online branding is like painting on a vast, limitless canvas. With many platforms, from websites to social media, brands can cast a wide net, reaching diverse audiences. The key is consistency. Each digital touchpoint, whether a tweet, a blog post, or an Instagram story, contributes to a unified narrative.

Selma revamped her website, ensuring that her brand's colors, logo, and messaging were uniform across all digital platforms. She authentically engaged with her online community, gathering feedback and weaving their stories into her brand's digital vibe.

Alternatively, she leveraged the power of storytelling through her blog, sharing the journey of her designs from sketch to finished product, the sustainable sources of her materials, and the artisans behind the scenes. In the vast expanse of the digital world, Selma's brand became a beacon of authenticity and transparency.

The Tangible Touchpoint

On the other hand, offline branding brings an element that the digital realm can't replicate: tangibility. It's in the feel of a product, the ambiance of a store, and the tone of face-to-face customer service. Every offline interaction is an opportunity to create a lasting sensory memory.

Selma transformed her pop-up shop into an experience. She ensured that her brand's colors painted the walls, and eco-friendly materials showcased the essence of sustainability. More importantly, she trained her team to echo the brand's ideology in every customer interaction, embodying the values she championed online.

She also organized events, intertwining her online and offline worlds. Workshops on sustainable fashion, meet-and-greets with her artisans, and community fashion shows became regular. Her physical space became an immersive hub, an extension of her digital brand brought to life.

The Harmonious Dance

As months passed, Selma witnessed the magic of integrated branding unfold. Customers would walk into her store, excitedly talking about a recent blog post or a captivating Instagram reel. The line between online and offline blurred, and her brand danced harmoniously between the two.

But Selma's journey wasn't without its challenges. Keeping pace with the ever-evolving digital landscape while maintaining a physical presence was demanding. Yet, the rewards—a loyal community, brand recognition, and amplified impact—made every effort worth it.

Branding in the Modern Age: A Symphony of Experiences

Today, Selma's brand is more than just a sustainable clothing line. It's an experience, a journey, a movement. Her story underscores the essence of modern branding: it's not about choosing between online and offline. It's about orchestrating a symphony of experiences, ensuring that each digital or tangible note resonates with harmony and purpose.

Building a brand in today's world is about recognizing the unique strengths of both the digital and tangible realms, weaving them into a narrative that captivates, inspires, and endures.

Consistency and Authenticity in Branding

In the crowded streets of Chicago, Jamie had a vision. She dreamed of a coffee shop, not just any coffee shop, but one that would be a haven for artists, writers, and dreamers alike. Her vision was crystal clear: vintage furniture, walls adorned with local art, and the soft hum of vinyl records playing in the background. It would be named "Retro Sip."

Yet, as Jamie ventured into the business realm, she learned that the intricacies of branding went far beyond the interior décor of her shop. She grappled with logos, taglines, social media, and customer experience. Consistently and authentically emerged as her guiding stars amid this swirl of branding elements.

The Power of Predictability: Consistency in Branding

Imagine visiting a McDonald's in Tokyo and then one in Paris. Despite the vast geographical and cultural differences, there's a comforting familiarity in the golden arches, the color scheme, and even the taste of the Big Mac. That's the power of brand consistency.

When Jamie opened the first Retro Sip, she poured her soul into every detail. The logo, a vintage vinyl record with a coffee cup in the center, was displayed proudly at the entrance and on every cup. The color palette of muted browns and creams was carefully chosen to evoke nostalgia.

As Retro Sip gained popularity and Jamie considered expansion, she realized the challenge was replicating the coffee's quality and the brand's soul in every new location. From the staff's uniforms to the Instagram posts, from the in-shop playlists to the loyalty cards, everything had to echo the Retro Sip vibe. The consistency was not just a visual or auditory experience, but an emotion. Whether they stepped into Retro Sip in Chicago, New York, or later in Los Angeles, customers felt the same warmth and artistic embrace.

Heart Over Hype: Authenticity in Branding

The digital age is an age of information abundance. Customers today are astute, discerning, and value-driven. They seek brands that don't just meet their needs but resonate with their beliefs. This is where authenticity plays a pivotal role.

Retro Sip wasn't just a business for Jamie; it was a statement. She believed in supporting local artists and providing a platform for their expression. True to this, every Retro Sip outlet became a canvas for local artists. Monthly art showcases, poetry readings, and open mics became the norm.

Furthermore, Jamie actively sought feedback and was transparent about her business practices. When a customer inquired about the source of her coffee beans, she shared the story of the small-scale South American farmers she partnered with. When another pointed out the environmental impact of coffee grounds, Retro Sip introduced a program to recycle used coffee grounds as garden compost.

This wasn't just strategic branding; it was Jamie's truth. And her customers felt it. They weren't just buying coffee but buying into Jamie's vision, passion, and authenticity.

The Magic When Consistency Meets Authenticity

Years later, as multiple Retro Sip outlets dotted the country, Jamie reflected on her branding journey. The seamless blend of consistency and authenticity created a brand that people didn't just recognize, but loved and advocated for.

Consistency ensured that the brand was recognizable and reliable. It built a subconscious trust. Every time a customer saw the Retro Sip logo or the familiar color palette, they knew the experience they were in for.

On the other hand, authenticity builds a conscious trust. Customers knew Retro Sip wasn't a faceless corporation, but Jamie's dream materialized. They believed in her vision, commitment to the community, and genuine business approach.

The Enduring Legacy of Trust

At its core, branding is about creating an enduring relationship with the customer. And like all enduring relationships, it's built on trust. In branding, this trust is cultivated through the twin pillars of consistency and authenticity.

Jamie's Retro Sip wasn't just a coffee shop. It was a testament to the fact that when a brand remains consistent in its promise and authentic in its delivery; it ceases to be just a business. It becomes a legacy, an emotion, a movement. In the cacophony of brands vying for attention, it's the consistent and authentic ones that etch a lasting place in the hearts of their audience.

Chapter 20

W e each have our own part to play in the sweeping production of life, dancing through it to the beat of our hopes, dreams, and struggles. Yet, even as we navigate our unique journey, we inevitably connect with others, like stars in a vast constellation, through relationships, camaraderie, and associations. Our experiences and well-being are shaped by the support network we create through human connections.

Imagine walking on a tightrope, high above the ground, with every step demanding precision and balance. The very thought may be dizzying. Now envision that there's a safety net below this tightrope ready to catch you if you stumble. The journey on the rope doesn't change, but the presence of the net offers reassurance and courage. Such is the role of a robust support network in the balancing act of life.

The Safety Net in Emotional Storms

Emotional resilience is not just about how we face adversity, but also about who stands beside us during those trying times. With its unpredictable twists, life can sometimes usher in periods of despair, loss, or confusion. In such moments, a kind word, a listening ear, or a comforting shoulder can make a difference. A support network is an anchor, providing stability in emotional upheavals and ensuring we never feel isolated in our struggles.

Victoria, a young artist, faced a challenge when galleries consistently rejected her work. She grappled with self-doubt, wondering if her artistic pursuits were mere pipe dreams. Her close-knit group of friends from her art school days rallied around her, offering encouragement, constructive feedback, and, most importantly, belief in her talent. Their support became the wind beneath her wings, propelling her forward even when the journey seemed bleak.

Guiding Stars in the Odyssey of Choices

Life presents us with many choices, from career decisions to personal crossroads. While the responsibility for these choices lies with us, a support network acts as a compass, offering perspectives, insights, and, sometimes, hard truths. These external viewpoints, distilled from our network's collective wisdom and experiences, can illuminate pathways we may have overlooked, guiding us toward informed decisions.

Take the case of Alex, a budding entrepreneur who grappled with the decision to pivot his startup's direction after initial setbacks. His mentors and peers from the industry, part of his professional network, provided invaluable advice, sharing their tales of pivots, failures, and eventual successes. Their collective insights influenced Alex's decision, helping him chart a new, promising trajectory for his venture.

The Wellspring of Growth and Inspiration

Beyond the tangible realms of emotional and decisional support, our network often becomes the fountainhead of inspiration and growth. Being surrounded by passionate, driven, and compassionate individuals can ignite our aspirations, pushing us to transcend our boundaries. The tales of triumph, perseverance, innovation, and kindness that echo in our network can inspire us to dream bigger, act bolder, and give generously.

An environmental activist, Liam drew immense inspiration from his community of eco-warriors. Their stories of grassroots movements, innovative solutions to sustainability, and relentless advocacy fueled Liam's drive. The collective vision of his network spurred him to initiate community-driven environmental projects that garnered nationwide attention.

Cultivating and Nurturing Your Network

Recognizing the value of a strong support network is the first step. The subsequent journey is about cultivating and nurturing these connections. Authenticity is the cornerstone here. Building genuine relationships rooted in trust, empathy, and mutual respect ensures the support network thrives. Engage in active listening, be present in moments of need, celebrate successes, and navigate challenges together. The web evolves in this give and take, becoming a dynamic force of collective strength.

While we may be dancing to our unique tune, we are never truly alone. The variety of human connections that envelop us is our most significant asset, safety net, guiding star, and wellspring of inspiration. As the African proverb beautifully articulates, "If you want to go fast, go alone. If you want to go far, go together." In life's journey, let's cherish and fortify our support networks, celebrating the profound power of togetherness.

Building and Nurturing Relationships

Relationships are the cornerstone of our existence. Whether it's the familial bond we share with our parents and siblings or the friendships we cultivate over laughter and tears, these connections influence our lives. They are our refuge in a storm, our cheerleaders on the sidelines, and sometimes the mirror that reflects our strengths and vulnerabilities. But how do we go about managing these connections? How do we ensure that they remain strong, vibrant, and enriching?

The Genesis of Genuine Bonds

Every relationship has a starting point. Sometimes, it's a chance encounter on a train; at other times, it's years spent together in school corridors. Regardless of the origin, the seeds of genuine relationships are sown in authenticity. In an age dominated by digital interactions and fleeting connections, being genuine might seem like a relic of the past. However, it's the very essence of meaningful bonds. We lay the groundwork for mutual respect and trust when we approach others with an open heart, vacant of pretenses or masks.

Aisha met Maria during a pottery class and introduced herself. Instead of small talk, they found themselves deep in conversation about their dreams, fears, and the beauty of imperfections in art and life. This genuine interaction marked the beginning of a lifelong friendship.

Cultivating the Garden of Trust

If authenticity is the seed, trust is the water that nourishes the relationship. Trust isn't built overnight. It's a delicate dance of reliability, understanding, and consistent efforts. It's about showing up when it matters, listening without judgment, and holding secrets close to one's heart.

Consider Jake and Evan. Their professional rivalry was known to all. However, when Evan faced personal challenges during a crucial project, Jake stepped in, not as a competitor but as a supportive colleague. This act, with no ulterior motive, became the cornerstone of their trust, transforming competitors into confidants.

The Colors of Adaptability

They say change is the only constant, and this holds in relationships too. As individuals grow, their beliefs, ambitions, and perspectives evolve. Herein lies the challenge and beauty of relationships. Adapting to each other's growth, giving space when needed, and embracing the new phases of life together add vibrant hues to the bond.

Nina and Lara were inseparable during college. Life took them to different continents, bringing about changes in their worlds. However, their yearly reunions were a testament to their adaptability. They celebrated their differences, learned from each other's experiences, and cherished the evolved versions of one another.

Rekindling the Flame

No matter how strong, every relationship faces its winter—periods of disconnect, misunderstandings, or monotony. These phases aren't signs of the relationship's frailty but opportunities to rekindle the bond. Returning down memory lane, recreating cherished moments, or spending quality time together can reignite the warmth.

When Ryan and Zoe, married for a decade, felt the spark fading, they embarked on a journey. Not just a vacation, but a trip to rediscover each other. They revisited the café where they first met, danced to their favorite song from yesteryears, and penned letters expressing their feelings. This intentional effort returned the magic, reminding them of their deep-rooted love.

The Symphony of Mutual Growth

Relationships aren't just about looking at each other but looking in the same direction. Encouraging each other's dreams, being the sounding board for ideas, and celebrating milestones together fosters mutual growth. A bond wherein both individuals evolve as partners or friends and as individuals is a relationship that stands the test of time.

William, an aspiring writer, and Debbie, a passionate photographer, are the perfect exemplars. Their weekends were spent in quaint cafés, where William penned stories inspired by Debbie's photographs. They critiqued, appreciated, and motivated each other, becoming successful in their careers and enriching their bond.

In life's grand picture, relationships are the tiles that add color, depth, and beauty. They require effort, patience, understanding, and tons of love. Like a plant that needs watering, sunlight, and care, relationships, too, need nurturing. In return, they blossom, providing shade, beauty, and solace. The famous saying goes, "The best things in life are the people we love, the places we've been, and the memories we've made along the way." So, let's cherish the journey of building and nurturing these invaluable bonds, celebrating the symphony of love and connection.

Leaning on Others and Being There for Them

In a world that often exalts the image of the lone wolf–the self-reliant and unyielding individual–we sometimes forget the intrinsic human need for connection, understanding, and mutual support. Our souls thrive not in isolation but in the company of others who share our joys, bear witness to our sorrows, and lift us when our spirits falter. This is the delicate dance of leaning on others and being there for them in return. It's a dance that, when mastered, enriches our lives and the lives of those around us in profound and lasting ways.

Imagine, if you will, a playground seesaw. There's you on one side, and on the other, a friend. The seesaw's equilibrium is maintained when both participants understand the give-and-take rhythm. Just as in life, there are moments when you're up, riding high on success, joy, or sheer thrill. Your friend might be down, grappling with challenges or heartaches in those moments. Then, inevitably, the roles reverse. This continual shift, this balance, forms the core of human relationships. It's about understanding that everyone has moments in the sun and nights of despair.

But how do we perfect this dance? How do we ensure that we lean without burdening and support without smothering?

Understanding the Rhythms of Life

It's vital to recognize and respect the rhythms of life. Just as seasons change, so do our circumstances. There will be times of summer when everything feels bright and cheerful and times of winter when the cold winds of challenges make us yearn for warmth. By grasping the concept of ups and downs, we are more tolerant of other people's feelings and more likely to share our own.

The Strength in Vulnerability

There's a common misconception that leaning on others is a sign of weakness. In reality, it takes immense strength to admit when we're struggling, to show our vulnerabilities, and to ask for help. Doing so gives us a chance to heal, and grow and empowers others to do the same. It's a silent acknowledgment that says, "I trust you with my story, with my pain."

Active Listening: A Gift of Presence

When someone leans on us, they're often not seeking solutions but understanding. Active listening, which involves concentrating, understanding, and responding to what the other person is saying, is one of our most precious gifts. It's about being fully present, making the other person feel seen, heard, and valued.

Boundaries: The Framework of Mutual Respect

Being there for someone doesn't mean losing oneself. Setting healthy boundaries ensures we don't drain ourselves emotionally or physically while we offer support. It's a reminder that while we walk together on this journey, we each have paths and paces.

Celebrate, Mourn, and Grow Together

Life is a combination of highs and lows; every moment is enriched when shared. Celebrate the achievements, no matter how small.

Mourn the losses, understanding that grief shared is grief halved. And in all these moments, we grow together, learning from each other's experiences and perspectives.

The Beauty of Reciprocity

The dance of leaning and supporting is most beautiful when there's reciprocity. It's not about keeping score, but understanding that a relationship thrives when both individuals can be pillars for each other. Today, it might be you offering a shoulder, and tomorrow, you might be the one seeking solace.

Leaning on others and being there for them is not just about mutual dependence, but mutual enrichment. It's about creating a blend of shared experiences entwined with threads of trust, understanding, and love. In this dance, there's no leader or follower. Just two individuals are moving together harmoniously to the timeless tune of human connection. This dance reminds us of a universal truth: We are not alone. And in the company of others, we find strength, solace, and the sublime joy of shared existence.

As we draw the curtains on this journey together, it's essential to recognize that the path to maturity is neither linear nor uniform. Each individual's voyage through young adulthood is as unique as their fingerprint, shaped by personal experiences, choices, and, most importantly, the lessons drawn from them.

Navigating young adulthood with resilience and grace doesn't mean you won't stumble or falter. It signifies that when you do, you'll rise stronger, wiser, and with a spirit undeterred. The challenges you face, the bridges you cross, and the mountains you climb are but chapters in your expansive story.

To every young adult reading this, remember: You have within you an immeasurable strength and limitless potential. Every experience, good or bad, is an opportunity to grow, evolve, and inch closer to the person you aspire to be.

As you continue on your unique journey, may you carry forward the lessons, insights, and stories shared on these pages. As the author, I hope my words have been a beacon, a comfort, and a source of encouragement. Keep pushing forward, keep learning, and most importantly, keep believing in yourself. The journey to maturity is just the beginning. Embrace it with all its intricacies, for it shapes the future of your life.

Here's to your journey, to the challenges you'll overcome, and to the incredible person you are becoming.

Afterword

T hank you for taking the time to read this book. Please use what you've just learned to take control of your future.

To help more readers find this book, please review the book wherever you've purchased it from.

To get more self-improvement resources and receive notifications for new book releases and podcast episodes, join Ben's newsletter by visiting,

www.TheSelfHelpCompany.com

About The Author

Ben Povlow was born in Philadelphia, PA. After growing up as an at-risk youth, while still a young adult, he continued to struggle to break free of his negative environment. He wanted a better life but didn't know how to achieve it. When he was twenty-eight years old, he became aware of self-help and personal development materials that would transform him in a way he never knew was possible.

Ben went on to improve the quality of his life by reading books, listening to audio trainings, and going to seminars of the most recognizable names in self-improvement. He followed these leaders around the country for several years, soaking up their knowledge and investing a lot of money into learning how to become the best version of himself he could be.

Ben believes we all have the power to change our circumstances through the way we think, act, and see ourselves. He has overcome many obstacles in his life and believes that if he can do it, anyone can.

He is now living the life of his dreams. He is married and lives with his wife, Kathi, and stepdaughter, Katelyn, in a quiet suburb in central North Carolina. Ben has committed himself to improving the lives of others by sharing his knowledge and experience. He is an inspiring motivational public speaker, a certified life coach, an author, and a business owner. You can learn more about Ben, his company, and services by visiting www.TheSelfHelpCompany.com